WAR ROOM

THE PEOPLE, TACTICS AND TECHNOLOGY BEHIND NARENDRA MODI'S 2014 WIN

ULLEKH NP

Dear RITU,
Best wishes. Hope you enjoy
the book.
Best
Ullekh

LOTUS COLLECTION
ROLI BOOKS

Lotus Collection

© Ullekh NP, 2015

First published in 2015

The Lotus Collection
An imprint of
Roli Books Pvt. Ltd
M-75, Greater Kailash II Market, New Delhi 110 048
Phone: ++91 (011) 40682000
Fax: ++91 (011) 2921 7185
E-mail: info@rolibooks.com
Website: www.rolibooks.com
Also at Bengaluru, Chennai, & Mumbai

Cover Design: Sneha Pamneja
Layout: Sunil Dutt
Production: Shaji Sahadevan

ISBN: 978-81-7436-998-7

Typeset in Garamond by Roli Books Pvt. Ltd.
Printed at Shree Maitrey Printech Pvt. Ltd., Noida.

To my father, the late Pattiam Gopalan
and my mother, NK Mridula

I begin with you.

CONTENTS

Foreword	*ix*
Prologue	3
Varanasi	7
The Shah of UP	19
Let the Hype Begin	36
War Room	52
NaMo	83
Opportunity Calling	105
Diaspora Power	126
Epilogue	136
Acknowledgements	*141*
Bibliography	*143*
Index	*144*

FOREWORD

In lucid prose, always precise never belaboured, Ullekh NP tells the story within the story of Modi's ample victory. The story itself is what all attentive Indians lived through: the words, deeds, images and media-reported events that made up the election campaign. It is a rich and varied story but it is not what interests the author.

What he investigates is the inside machinery that produced the sounds and imagery of the campaign and even more, the inside politics that aligned national and local politicians with Modi's trajectory to power, securing their fullest support if possible, their partial support if necessary, or at least their grudging respect and desistence.

When it comes to his investigative flair and persistence, readers might be most amused – as well as instructed – by his layer-by-layer uncovering of the true author of the hugely popular slogan *Ab ki baar Modi sarkaar,* which was claimed by all manner of worthies and even a tycoon, before it was prosaically revealed that it was the adman who created the ad, that is Piyush Pandey, executive chairman and creative director at Ogilvy & Mather, who in turn attributed his success in selling Modi to Modi himself: "a fantastic product".

At a much deeper level, but always in light, fast, very readable prose, Ullekh probes the fundamental reason for Modi's sweeping victory. He starts with the plain fact that his predecessor, Manmohan

Singh, was not a fully empowered prime minister. That India with her immense diversities and multi-layered decentralization needs a PM who can really lead and powerfully, is obvious enough. But what it had under Singh was much less: "Without doubt, the institution... had lost its lustre under Singh as he waited for instructions from Sonia Gandhi. The role of the prime minister has been crucial for reforms. This was evident in the case of Narasimha Rao in 1991-1996 and AB Vajpayee in 1998-2004. But by 2011-12, the National Advisory Council (NAC), headed by Sonia Gandhi, had become an alternative power centre that was more powerful than the PMO. The casualty, of course, was governance."

That in turn lead to the wilting of the economy: "Under Singh, expenditure and economic activity started shrinking. Employment generation, too, was slow. So was growth in manufacturing, which fell in several quarters in the last years of [his government]."

Ullekh explains how the lack of leadership directly damaged investment, the very engine of growth:

"The low-profile Manmohan Singh would... never put his foot down when powerful Cabinet colleagues thrust indiscreet policies upon the government. The move to tax overseas companies for transactions that they had entered into in India in the past also shattered investor confidence in the Indian economy. One of the companies... was the biggest foreign corporate investor in India, Vodafone. The tax department sent Vodafone a tax bill of Rs 3,200 crore for allegedly undervaluing the shares Vodafone issued to its parent company. The tax department said that this difference in valuation was in fact a disguised loan subject to transfer pricing provisions. Vodafone argued that share premium is a capital receipt, not income and hence not taxable. The case stretched on so long, it scared off potential overseas investors."

Weak leadership also crippled the engine of economic growth in other ways: "[there was a]... reluctance in giving clearances to such projects by the environment ministry under Jairam Ramesh first and then under Congress leader Jayanthi Natarajan, who faced unconfirmed charges of soliciting bribes for clearing projects. She had to finally step down from the ministerial post in early 2014 for, it appeared, delaying of projects for months without giving any plausible reason. By the time the seniors in the party took note and intervened, such criminal negligence of aborting new projects had done major damage to the Indian economy, already wobbling under the weight of deteriorating investor sentiment."

Ullekh finally uncovers the deepest layer of the preference for 'starving the goose that lays the golden eggs' ideology:

"Even when Singh's government (or rather Sonia's) returned to power in 2009 without the Left, it continued to "put a lot of emphasis on social spending... Here was an opportunity to put the country back on the reform track. But [instead there was a] consistent expansion of its key entitlement-focused schemes...."

And the problem, of course, was that the ideology was wrong. Yes, when the Vodafones and all the others are given breathing room, when they are not crushed by taxes, the goose becomes fatter and fatter, so that the poor look even thinner next to it. *But there are fewer of them* – the number of poor keeps going down even as the rich become richer, and that is the central truth that matters. Ullekh presents this analysis via the most authoritative of voices, the globally known Indian economist Jagdish Bhagwati: "[He]..explained to me in an interview in late 2012 that Manmohan Singh's hands were tied by the peculiar nature of governance in place, referring to remote controlling of the running of his government by Congress President Sonia Gandhi.... His (Singh's) ability to deliver reforms is handicapped by the fact that the people in favour of track-II reforms (social spending, et cetera) around Ms Gandhi are not appreciative of the fact that track-I reforms (growth-oriented initiatives) are absolutely necessary, that we need to intensify and broaden them to continue making a direct impact on poverty and generating revenues (for welfare schemes)... Bhagwati was very critical of economists who had lauded Singh's policies. A lot of them (even luminaries such as Amartya Sen and Mahbub-ul-Haq) used to say that growth wouldn't influence poverty."

Ultimately it really is as simple as that: what the poor need is wealth, and wealth must be created before it can be redistributed.

That is what Modi is all about: economic growth by any feasible method, from road-building to cutting back the License Raj. Ullekh is always objective as he gives the blow-by-blow account of how Modi won the election. Along with his fellow Indians, he wants results, and soon.

– Edward N. Luttwak
Chevy Chase, Maryland, US
October 2014

Edward N. Luttwak *is a renowned American military historian, strategist and a political scientist. A Cold Warrier, he is the author of best-selling books such as* The Grand Strategy of the Roman Empire; The Grand Strategy of the Byzantine Empire; *and* The Grand Strategy of the Soviet Union. *His latest book is* The Rise of China vs. the Logic of Strategy.

"I promise you, in the 21st century Narendra Modi will never become the prime minister of the country… But if he wants to distribute tea here, we will find a place for him."

– Congress leader Mani Shankar Aiyar at a high-level meet of his party on 16 January 2014

PROLOGUE

Elections in the world's largest democracy have never been a tepid affair. In 2014, they saw unprecedented participation – in both voting and campaigning – by India's thriving middle classes. Driven by the idea of modernity and the winds of political change around the world, voters across the social spectrum were eager to exercise their choice in a country that prides itself on its vibrant democratic history, the highlight of which is the general election held every five years.

These, expectedly, are a study in the art of hype. The sheer numbers of India's democratic machinery are staggering and the frenzy on the street during election time surpasses that of the world's biggest carnivals. At the time of the general election in 2014, India was home to over eighty-one crore eligible voters, which is more than the population of all of Europe. All major political parties – the country of 1,600-plus languages and dialects has more than 1,500 large and small parties – were prepared to pack a punch.

Politics anywhere is an exercise in selling, and the value of promotion in India is much enhanced thanks to the enormity and diversity of its voters. Sample this: the state of Uttar Pradesh (UP) has 13.4 crore voters, the largest number of eligible voters of all states in the country. It showcases the best and worst of India. Caste, religion, rural-urban divide, gender and numerous other variables decide who wins and who loses – and political parties, including those in the 'secular' Left, vie with one another to retain or encroach onto new vote banks. Meanwhile, critics claim that the increasing influence of the corporate sector that lavishly funds political parties has distorted India's secular political traditions; for their part, libertarians claim the system is skewed in favour of an ill-informed, uneducated majority.

Whatever its flaws, the system continues to flourish and inspire innovation. This time around, the elections acquired a techie halo. More than 65 percent of India's population is aged thirty-five or under; half its people are under twenty-five; and 2.3 crore new Indian voters are in the age group of 18-19. These young people are increasingly wired and hungry for information from around the world – which is now accessible to a sizeable chunk of them on little devices in their hands. After all, more people in the second fastest-growing major economy in the world have access to mobile phones than toilets. Reaching out to these citizens through the use of new technology was far more imperative in this general election than ever before.

Packaging a political candidate in electronic gloss and glamour – with a figurative satin bow on top – was vital this time to capture the imagination of its huge chunk of young voters. For the first time, social media tools from Twitter, Facebook, WhatsApp and Google Hangout to web-pages and even Smartphone apps that help women track their menstrual cycles, were put to extensive use by political campaign managers. For the first time, the country's only prime ministerial candidate, who routinely drew lakhs of people to his rallies, also spoke as a holographic image in 3D rallies held at close to 150 locations simultaneously.

In a break from tradition, elections this time were more presidential by nature and less parliamentary – in a presidential system like the US, one nominee of each leading party is projected as the leader. In contrast, in a parliamentary system such as India, typically, voters select their party of choice, which then selects its own leader once it wins. Of course, voters, spread across 9.3 lakh polling booths, still had to elect 543 members to the Parliament. But this time, the campaign was so personality-driven that it was made to look like a fight between Narendra Modi, the prime ministerial candidate of the Bharatiya Janata Party (BJP), versus Rahul Gandhi, the Congress vice-president, who opted to be its chief campaigner but not prime ministerial candidate.

Led by a team of techies and fresh graduates armed with PCs, laptops, headphones, iPads and spunky ideas, the no-holds-barred political campaign saw Modi staying several notches high, all through, in a massive five-week election carried out in ten phases starting on 8 April and ending on 12 May 2014. The number of volunteers enlisted by Team Modi to drive home his message – and the storm of hype about him – far outnumbered those of his nearest rival. For the first time, the poll campaign was designed to a fault, assisted largely by an animated bunch of outsiders attracted and dazzled by the fantasy of Modi the messiah. Modi's party was bolstered by the 24x7 support of these spirited volunteers, many of whom gave up high-paying professional jobs motivated by the desire to see their beloved Modi*ji* win. Driven by the idea of change, development and economic growth, they zealously recruited thousands more like-minded volunteers at the grassroots level to the Modi cause, something that even the BJP could not have predicted or planned.

Yes, Candidate Modi made a splash and exuded the power of a reformer India was longing for, but the process by which his publicists went about magnifying the lure of that persona manifold in the crucial months ahead of the polls is destined to become part of the country's election lore. This book will describe the scale and scope of the blitzkrieg that launched Modi.

It was a perfect pitch, tailored to project the man as an idea whose time had come. And it worked.

1 VARANASI

"Withdrawn from the taint of senses, abiding in peace, holy with the flowing waters of the great Manikarnika and the sacred Ganga, the source of light and liberation, the blessed Kashi am I."

— Jagat Guru Adi Shankaracharya

A
t dawn on 17 March 2014, the day of the annual Holi festival, Varanasi looked as cheerfully filthy as ever. All the litter in the world had found its graveyard in the narrow alleys leading to Kedar Ghat, where one had to wade through a cloud of ganja and a maze of men and women in stupor, lying as if they were dead next to their begging bowls, sticks and cheap plastic bottles of water. The fresh air that the great saint Adi Shankara had loved about this place was not what I breathed when I took the walk down the steep steps of the ghat to meet a beaming boatman. It was 4 a.m. and our ride down the river Ganga alongside some of the shrines considered holiest by Hindus and the already active riverfront was exhilarating in a strange, philosophical way.

In a few months the Ganga was going to be the perfect backdrop for the stunning victory celebrations of an unlikely winner, and later the highlight of his rock-star moment at New York's Madison Square Garden where he exhorted the Indian-American community to help save the dying river of life.

By the time I got back from my whimsical meanderings, it was 7 a.m. and the festival of colour was yet to begin with a bang. Make that *bhang* (marijuana) in milk. Mischief-makers had their fill of day-long debauchery, mostly by targeting outsiders not used to the excesses typical of a day in the world's oldest living city, in India's most populous state of Uttar Pradesh. From my hotel room window, I saw two female Japanese tourists fleeing from a group of Holi hooligans and was overcome by a forlorn sense of guilt and disgust until I was distracted by a call from Ajay Rai, the local muscle man, who would soon be named the Congress nominee from the Varanasi Lok Sabha seat. Nobody splashed colours when his assistant Kundan Singh ferried me to Rai's home on a scooter. Rai, awash in the colours of Holi himself, flexed his facial and arm muscles as he dwelt on why he was the right candidate to outwrestle Narendra Modi, the rival Bharatiya Janata Party's prime ministerial candidate. "Modi doesn't know a thing about Varanasi," Rai told me. "His team and party are a confused lot – they know I know the local dynamics more."

Rai hoped that the Gandhis, the First Family of the 129-year-old Congress party, would presently endorse his candidature to take on Modi in what was shaping into one of the most pathbreaking elections – or perhaps the most important – in recent Indian history. "This is *my* Varanasi. He is an outsider who knows nothing about this city's people. I can finish him off here," Rai thundered with a Mike Tysonesque flair. BJP posters lining the religious city's crumbling, dirty walls shrieked 'Har Har Modi' in a fervour of comparison with Lord Shiva himself – hailed by devotees with the chant, 'Har Har Mahadev'. Rai rubbished such outrageous similes, sensing that his argument would click in a city long affiliated with the god. "Who is Modi to compare himself to Mahadev? Is he saying he is Lord Shiva?" taunted Rai.

For someone who was a former BJP leader himself, Rai would have known only too well that the Modi campaign team was not in the least bit confused, its slogans far from accidental, its volunteers anything but dawdling. Rai's blustering bravado sixty-four days before polling in Varanasi gave away the underlying nervousness that the 'Idea of Modi' – carefully crafted and meticulously executed – had evoked in rivals.

***

Varanasi, which is older than Jerusalem and Athens, continues to be one of Hinduism's holiest cities. Maddeningly dirty, yet undeniably holy, Varanasi (also called Benaras) is bound to fascinate any political party that espouses the 'Hindu religious' cause. It is still a hotbed for upper-caste politics. Though the rest of the state of Uttar Pradesh has, in recent years, seen a shattering of caste hierarchies and the dismantling of Brahmin dominance in most parts, you can still find deep roots of the old ways in Varanasi.

But political affiliations have changed drastically. In the 1980s, the late Congress veteran Kamalapati Tripathi managed to stay in power using his ties with the Brahmins of Varanasi, a powerful high-caste group of opinion leaders that continues to handle the affairs of various affluent temples and wields tremendous influence among Hindu voters. The Ram Janmabhoomi agitation of the late 1980s and the early 1990s changed equations. The agitation called for building a temple in the name of Lord Ram in place of a disputed sixteenth-century mosque at Ayodhya built by Babar, the invader-emperor who founded the Mughal dynasty in India. According to the ancient Hindu scriptures, Ram – one of the supreme Hindu gods – is believed to have been born in Ayodha eons ago. The BJP-led agitation to destroy the Babri Mosque and set up a Ram Temple kicked up religious passion across the country and especially in the Hindi belt (a collective term for parts of northern and central India where Hindi is the predominant language), suddenly catapulting BJP to the mainstream. Since then, the BJP has made deep inroads in this town, winning it in all Lok Sabha elections since 1991 with the exception of 2004.

And yet, despite its firm hold on Varanasi, the BJP of the twenty-first century did not hold sway in most of the state of Uttar Pradesh, which sends eighty lawmakers to the Indian Parliament, the single highest figure from any state. In fact, in mid-2013, a resounding poll win in Uttar Pradesh looked near impossible for the BJP what with the Samajwadi Party (SP) and the Bahujan Samaj Party (BSP), two powerful regional parties in the state, walking away with votes from the majority of castes here. The SP, led by former socialist leader and former Chief Minister Mulayam Singh Yadav, had monopolised the

Other Backward Caste (OBC) and Muslim votes. The BSP, headed by former Chief Minister Mayawati, had assured itself of both the lowest (the Dalits) and the highest end (the Brahmins) of the Hindu caste spectrum in positions of power.

With the majority of Hindus – the OBCs and Dalits – veering towards the SP and the BSP, and practically no Muslims on its side, the BJP was left with few takers. The party had fared poorly in the elections in the state for more than a decade, winning only ten of the eighty Lok Sabha seats in the 2009 general election, infuriatingly lower than their majority tally of fifty-eight in 1998. For BJP to form a government at the Centre, the state of UP was indispensable. The nationalist party would have to recapture lost ground.

It was time for BJP's Big Brother to make a move.

***

The Rashtriya Swayam Sevak Sangh (RSS), founded in 1925 by Dr Keshav Baliram Hedgewar to uphold and spread Hindutva (a nationalist form of Hinduism) and expanded nationwide by his highly shrewd successor Madhav Sadashiv Golwalkar, was ready to help resurrect the BJP, its political arm. RSS is known to run more than 40,000 *shakhas* (branches) across the country, training lakhs of young men. The morning meetings of the *shakhas* involve physical exercise and play and are organised for an hour in public places every day. RSS volunteers are also trained in civil work and relief operations. Though banned twice since freedom for being 'anti-national', the religious group had been invited to take part in the Republic Day parade of 1963 in recognition of its volunteer work during the war with China the previous year. Although the RSS itself is avowedly a social organisation, its vice-like grip on India's parliamentary and legislative forums is ensured by its political arm, the BJP.

RSS leaders were aware that long spells of being out of power at the national level were demoralising the cadre and hurting the strength of the organisation in crucial states, such as UP and Bihar where infighting and desertion became rampant. BJP and its allies – a rainbow coalition of like-minded, largely centre-Right parties who call themselves National Democratic Alliance (NDA) – had not been in the hot seat of national politics for meaningful stretches of time. Having suffered a humiliating defeat at the hustings in a high-voltage campaign in 2004 and later in 2009 to the United Progressive Alliance (UPA) – the Congress-led coalition of largely centre-Left entities – the BJP was in bad shape.

The thought – how to get the BJP toned up for the decisive poll bout of 2014 – had been on the collective minds of the Sangh leadership for long. They discussed the subject threadbare as early as 15 March 2013, when these leaders met in Jaipur for an RSS Pratinidhi Sabha meeting. Several senior members of the BJP, including Arun Jaitley, Rajnath Singh and others, had already impressed upon the Sangh leadership, especially Sarsanghchalak Mohan Bhagwat, the need for a campaign spearhead.

The BJP's goal was to best the ruling UPA party in a tit-for-tat, aggressive campaign and continuously wrest the political narrative of the moment in the run-up to the polls. And Uttar Pradesh alone could swing political fortunes in its favour. The BJP had to reboot, all big hitters agreed.

***

After all, the time was ripe to shove the Congress out of power. Never had India's GOP (grand old party) looked so vulnerable and shaken. The first time it was out of power was after the elections of 1977, when people voted for change, horrified by the Emergency imposed by then Prime Minister Indira Gandhi to clamp down on massive anti-government protests and silence her detractors within and outside the Congress. The second rout came in 1989, when the Congress was buffeted by the strong winds of the Bofors arms deal. Geneva-based journalist Chitra Subramaniam broke an explosive news report that people close to the then Prime Minister Rajiv Gandhi (son of Indira) received illegal kickbacks for swinging an arms deal in favour of Swedish company Bofors AB for the purchase of guns for the Indian army. The revelation erupted into a major corruption scandal and brought down Rajiv Gandhi's government. The third time, in 1996, the general election took place in the shadow of more corruption scandals that led to the exit of seven Cabinet ministers in the Congress-led minority government of PV Narasimha Rao and resulted in the ruling party being plagued by factionalism and splits. Though its poor show continued in the 1998 and 1999 polls, the Congress-led UPA returned to power in 2004 to stay afloat for a decade, during which time its popularity declined rapidly after a series of in-your-face corruption scandals were unearthed (*see* Chapter 6).

Delhi-based psephologist Devendra Kumar, who had compared party performance and mood of the nation prior to the elections of 1977, 1989 and 1996, notes that the Congress' organisation and slogans were never as weak and unappealing as they were in the 2014 polls. If BJP had to strike, the time was now.

***

Picking a new leader who could lead the BJP from the front meant ringing out the old. That meant hurting the sensitivities of a few veteran leaders within the party fold. Despite these worries, at the March 2013 RSS meet, it didn't take long for RSS chief Bhagwat to weigh the pros and cons and arrive at an internal decision: Narendra Modi, who had led the BJP to three successive victories in Gujarat and had earned – whether it was thanks to his own publicity apparatus or not – a name for himself as a man of words and deeds, would lead the national poll campaign.

Mohan Bhagwat had never been a great fan of Modi's, especially after the latter became Gujarat's chief minister in 2001 and refused to accept writs from the Sangh or its feeder organisations, notably the Bharatiya Mazdoor Sangh (the trade-union arm of the RSS), on labour-related and other issues, and forged ahead with the chief executive officer-like functioning he is known for now. That Modi and Bhagwat were not the best of friends was well-known, but, to their credit, neither Bhagwat nor the RSS let such misgivings affect their choice of the man who should lead the BJP to a much-needed victory, and to re-energise the organisation rendered hollow and largely ineffective in the fallow years when it was out of power at the national level. The RSS leadership was excited about the public perception that Modi was a moderniser and leader with tremendous reformist zeal.

Soon after this meeting, which internally concluded that Modi would lead the BJP in the 2014 general election, Bhagwat entrusted two senior RSS functionaries, Bhaiyyaji Joshi and Suresh Soni, with the task of conveying the decision to senior BJP leaders, some of whom were opposed to the move of elevating Modi to lead the party's national poll campaign. There were murmurs of dissent. However, within a few months, at the 8 June 2013 National Executive meeting of the BJP held in Goa, the decision was made public: Modi was named the chief campaigner of the BJP. In the coming months, the RSS had to spring to action to get Modi anointed as more than just the chief campaigner.

Modi would have to be the prime ministerial candidate as well.

But then, there was another leader – Modi's one-time mentor – who had been nursing prime ministerial ambitions for long. And this was his last opportunity. He was already eighty-six.

LK Advani, the high-profile deputy prime minister and Union home minister in the NDA government of 1999-2004 and one of the BJP's founder-leaders along with former Prime Minister AB Vajpayee, had always languished as number two in the shadow of the far more charismatic Vajpayee. Advani hoped Modi would relent if he put his foot down. After all, in 2002 when Vajpayee indicated that Modi step down as chief minister in the aftermath of the mindless communal riots in Gujarat, it was Advani who came to Modi's rescue (*see* Chapter 5). Surely, Modi would return the favour now?

But Advani's hopes were misplaced.

On 13 September 2013, Advani was about to leave for the BJP Parliamentary Board meeting at the Ashoka Road headquarters of the BJP from his Prithviraj Road residence around 3 p.m. when he received a call from Nitin Gadkari who had been directed by the party leadership that a decision on Modi as PM candidate could not be delayed any longer. Advani was crestfallen, but knew that he had to yield. Sushma Swaraj, Advani's protégé, raised her objections to Modi becoming the PM candidate at the Parliamentary Board meeting, but was shot down by BJP stalwarts Arun Jaitley, N Venkaiah Naidu and Thawarchand Gehlot. Soon, she too fell in line – in the press conference held soon afterwards, Swaraj sat next to Modi in an apparent show of solidarity. BJP President Rajnath Singh then announced that support for Modi was unanimous.

Advani did not attend the Parliamentary Board meeting.

For his part, the prime ministerial nominee himself announced that he would seek Advani's blessings. On cue, within hours, Madhya Pradesh Chief Minister Shivraj Chauhan and Chhattisgarh's Raman Singh, both BJP leaders, threw their weight behind Modi through tweets.

***

When a balding man with sharp eyes and stout build arrived in Varanasi in early June of 2013 as part of a recce suggested by the RSS, it didn't take him long to report back that Varanasi, the ancient temple city, was the ideal seat from across India for Modi to contest from. Amit Shah recognised Varanasi as a pivotal constituency that would help generate a cascade of support for the BJP, especially in the Poorvanchal region, which comprises twenty-two districts of eastern Uttar Pradesh, and parts of the neighbouring state of Bihar. The idea was to kick off a trend in Varanasi by invoking faith and Hindutva sentiments. The candidature of Modi, feted as an alpha Hindu male, would reenergise the cadres of the BJP, which had weakened in the region over the years thanks to the rise of regional entities such as the SP and the BSP.

Shah, a relentless, ruthlessly driven organiser of the BJP and Modi's comrade for thirty-three years, had been instrumental in battering the Congress in Gujarat in a meticulous way. While the RSS was busy convincing the BJP leadership to accept Modi as their poster boy, it had also assigned Shah the homework of identifying a seat in the Hindi heartland for him. Which means the decision to field Modi from Varanasi was taken by the RSS months before his being nominated the prime ministerial candidate, and more than nine months before the public announcement of his candidature from the holy city. Senior journalist PR Ramesh had reported in *The Economic Times* as early as July 2013 that Modi would contest from Varanasi and that the incumbent from the temple town, veteran BJP leader and former Union minister Murli Manohar Joshi, would be allotted another seat in Uttar Pradesh. "The logic was clear: Modi contesting from Varanasi would result in a wave of sorts that would sweep across Poorvanchal, a region that was pivotal enough for the party to increase its tally in the Hindi belt and come to power in the Centre," Union minister Dharmendra Pradhan, who was in charge of elections in Bihar, told me during the poll campaign.

There was still a minor problem at hand: Joshi, the sitting MP from Varanasi, kept arguing for retaining the seat. The eighty-year-old former BJP president had shifted base to Varanasi after he lost from the Allahabad Lok Sabha seat in 2004, after three successive wins there. The ghats of Benaras had been auspicious for him. Then, on the evening of 13 March 2014, Amit Shah drove down to his Raisina Road residence in New Delhi to say that he had only one choice: contest from Kanpur or not contest at all.

After Advani, it was Joshi's turn to give in.

On 15 March 2014, Modi was formally announced the BJP candidate from Varanasi. It was exactly one year after the RSS had zoomed in on their golden boy.

***

By Holi two days later, Dr Krishna Gopal, an RSS leader with astute knowledge of the region and culture, besides being a scholar in Dalit literature from the state, had already been camping in Uttar Pradesh for three months, closely monitoring the Varanasi constituency. Gopal was a man on a mission. With long experience of working in the state, he had been dispatched there by the RSS high command to keep a tab on the campaign and to stem infighting that was rampant among BJP leaders. The leadership wanted Gopal to leave nothing to chance, and he insisted on feedback from local leaders of each constituency on the winnability factor of candidates recommended by them.

With his spectacles, moustache and salt-and-pepper hair, Gopal's serious, no-nonsense demeanour in those days reflected the arduousness of his task: to end the monopoly of very senior BJP leaders in ticket distribution, which often meant that backward caste leaders were under-represented. He had already conducted numerous mass-contact programmes, and set up cadre-based squads to ensure voter turnout – there are more than seventeen lakh registered voters in Varanasi – and to manage poll booths.

The RSS leaders I met several times in the run-up to the 12 May election in Varanasi were consistent about Modi's victory margin from the start: more than three and a half lakh votes, they predicted. There was talk that Modi's OBC push was alienating upper-caste voters who were expected to throw their weight behind Congress' Rai. The road-shows by Modi's most vocal opponent – former Delhi Chief Minister Arvind Kejriwal, the diminutive, bespectacled IITian who became an anti-graft crusader and then a star victor in the Delhi assembly elections of December 2013 – gave the impression that Kejriwal may do to Modi in Varanasi what he did to former Delhi Chief Minister Sheila Dikshit in Delhi: trounce him. Kejriwal had entered the fray in Varanasi after holding a popular referendum, adding to the drama and polemics he was usually known for. A section of the media even forecast the Varanasi poll combat to be a cliffhanger of a fight for Modi. "Modi will bite the dust," Kejriwal told me a day before the vote.

The Aam Aadmi Party (AAP) leader was eyeing support from the Muslims of the constituency. In the minds of some three lakh Muslim voters in Varanasi, the image of Modi from the 2002 riots in Gujarat is fresh – all non-BJP parties ensure that it remains so, portraying the BJP heavyweight as a butcher of Muslims. Muslim vote is considered crucial, and combined with Dalit votes, it is a stunning combination in this Lok Sabha seat. In the 2009 elections, BJP's Joshi won by a narrow margin of 17,000 votes while the runner-up Mukhtar Ansari, who was then with the BSP, pulled in a good chunk of Dalit and Muslim voters to put up a good fight. Some Muslim community leaders contend that Ansari would have become the MP (Member of Parliament), if the BJP had not played the communal card and appealed to Dalits not to elect a Muslim because the MP from the constituency gets nominated to the management of the famous Kashi Vishwanath temple. An RSS leader admitted to me that it was a "last-minute strategy" adopted by the Sangh to "save Joshi*ji*", seen as an outsider. "A Muslim should not be given a chance to be part of running our most holy temple. That was our argument. And it worked," he says.

While there was excitement among Hindus about Modi's candidature – a good chunk of them also bought into Modi's development agenda, arguing that Modi would bring the metro to this highly congested city – Muslim voters were mostly anxious. Some of them I spoke to were worried that the politics he would bring to Varanasi bode ill for non-Hindus. Ajmal, a trader on Madanpura Road, said, "He has a history of being anti-Muslim and has shown no sympathy to those who perished in the 2002 riots," emphasising that there was a feeling of deep insecurity among the Muslims. However, away from this middle-class neighbourhood, in the back alleys of Bada Bazaar, densely populated by poor Muslims, Jalaluddhin, a grocer, said he wasn't scared about "Modi coming to Varanasi". He wouldn't vote for him, though. "He is coming here after having built a huge position for himself at the national level, and there is nobody here who can take him on. What he should keep in mind, therefore, since he is going to win anyway is that he must treat all as equal, Hindu or Muslim. He must change," Jalaluddhin suggested.

Certainly, it was the Muslim fear or contempt towards Modi that Kejriwal tried to tap. Modi's road show on 24 April 2014 from the famous Banaras Hindu University (BHU) to the BJP office five kilometres away had turned the city into an ocean of saffron, revealing a militant behaviour inherent to the RSS. Such display of pro-Hindu identity was enough to scare the minorities in the city. Muslim representation at the Kejriwal road show, held on 9 May, was proof of such fears. Kejriwal and AAP members succeeded in creating a grand illusion of high popularity – people turned up in hordes to watch the former Delhi chief minister take a dip in the Ganga, walk through Varanasi's narrow roads exchanging pleasantries with the common man, and speak, poking fun at Modi's extravagant chopper trips. Kejriwal tore through Modi all through the campaign, targeting him for not raising pertinent issues.

But RSS and BJP leaders publicly dismissed Kejriwal's electoral challenge as a hiccup.

Towards the end of the campaign, despite the storm that Kejriwal had kicked up in Varanasi, RSS leaders still forecasted the margin of victory as upwards of 3.5 lakh votes. Varanasi went to the polls on 12 May, in the final phase of the Lok Sabha election following loud calls from local newspaper columnists month after month asking Modi to apologise to Muslims if he ever wanted to be prime minister. "We are prepared enough to know this is going to be a very smooth sail," an RSS leader from Varanasi said, emphasising that "the hard work that has gone behind is so huge that no election was fought before on this scale and enormity. We have ensured a Modi wave."

Modi polled 5,81,022 votes, securing 56.37 percent of the votes polled in the constituency. The runner-up Arvind Kejriwal got 2,09,238 votes. Ajay Rai got 75,614.

Modi's margin of victory: 3.71 lakh votes.

2 | THE SHAH OF UP

"If I had listened to my critics then I would not have done anything in my life."

– Amit Shah, in an interview to Rediff.com

I met Amit Shah over breakfast along with two senior journalists in a hotel room far too posh for the decrepit town of Muzaffarnagar, UP. It was a hot, sticky morning in April 2014 and the central air-conditioning was the star of the moment. Several of Shah's comrades waited in throne-like chairs in the ornate lounge outside while he genially served us carrot *parathas*, mildly sweet and delicious, white bread and butter, and tea. Like any gracious Indian host, he encouraged us to eat more as he tucked into the *parathas* with gusto. When we resisted, he advised us that one should eat more in the morning and less at lunchtime and dinner. He preferred a heavy breakfast, he said, which also included several kinds of fruit, *idli* and *vada*. When we finally got to the business of talking about the challenges in Uttar Pradesh for the BJP, he came up with an early UP tally for his party: 38-40 seats out of 80. He had been travelling extensively in UP since early 2012, more than a year before he was made the central leader in charge of the UP unit of the BJP on 12 June 2013, to explore how the Samajwadi Party had managed to secure a stunning victory in the 2012 assembly polls in the state. Even as we talked, his colleagues outside shifted in their feet as they waited to give him the latest updates from the ground.

By early 2013, Shah had been shuttling back and forth between Delhi and Uttar Pradesh's forlorn villages almost without a break, he told us. Mostly a reluctant interviewee, he was so excited to meet a few regional journalists from southern India in a far-flung area of western UP that he immediately gave them an interview, despite having decided not to do so during that period. He was deeply impressed by the fact that some journalists were ready to go the extra mile – and in this case several hundred miles – something that he invariably did as a matter of course.

Our conversation was often interrupted by myriad beeps from at least five mobile phones in his possession, all handled by one of his dutiful assistants whose job profile included alerting Shah about the time for his shot of insulin. A diabetic, Shah however never let any physical weakness hurt his tireless campaigning through Uttar Pradesh's badlands, where lawlessness was the rule more than the exception, where power supply was a luxury more than a basic amenity, where might was right, where violence against Dalits and women was a daily occurrence and perpetrators mostly walked away unscathed.

Born in 1964 in Mumbai (he says Wikipedia got it wrong when it entered his birthplace as Chicago), Shah joined his father Anilchandra Shah's PVC pipe business and dabbled in stock trading after graduating with a B.Sc. degree in biochemistry. A diehard family man, the BJP president is married to Sonal*ben*; the couple have a son, Jay, and live in Delhi's Jangpura neighbourhood. Shah has been Modi's comrade-in-arms for over three decades. The two had met in 1982 when Modi was an RSS *pracharak* and Shah was just seventeen years old. It was a brotherhood in saffron that was meant to last. In fact, when the late RSS Sarsanghchalak Balasaheb Deoras asked Modi to join the BJP, Shah was one of the few people with whom Modi shared his doubts about the likely role. "[Modi] was initially reluctant," remembers Shah. "'How can a square peg fit into a round hole?' was his worry."

Uber-geek Dr. Vijay Chauthaiwale, molecular biologist and former vice-president (discovery research) at Torrent Pharmaceuticals, whom Modi had roped in to help the 'Delhi war room' housed at the Ashoka Road office of the BJP, had closely watched Shah all through the 2014 poll and marvels at his keen political acumen and drive. He remembers Shah rushing back from Uttar Pradesh to attend crucial poll-related meetings of the party in Delhi, and as soon as they were over, he would return to western UP. In the first few phases of polls, he would travel by car to the dust and grime of Muzaffarnagar, reaching there around 1 a.m. Then he would discuss polls with party workers, collecting information, throwing instructions, ticking them off and coming up with fresh ideas until 4.30 a.m. The entire team would then sleep at the office till 10.30–11 a.m., followed by his usual big breakfast. Shah would return to Delhi in the steaming hot north Indian afternoon to make plans for eastern UP where polls were due in later phases.

The BJP in Uttar Pradesh was a dormant giant, one symptom of which was that it had not contested panchayat elections for the past ten years because of fear of defeat. It was Shah who shook the party organisation out of its slumber. In the months after he plunged into the national campaign, he became intensely familiar with all nuances of running the party. According to Chauthaiwale, Shah knew close to 100 BJP local leaders in each Lok Sabha constituency of Uttar Pradesh by name. His memory of places and people, BJP leaders from the state say, was elephantine. "We have heard that Julius Caesar used to know the names of most of his soldiers. Shah*ji* was blessed with similar memory. In the 2014 elections, he was really a Caesar-like presence in the states," one of them told me.

Shah was instrumental in cobbling an alliance with an Uttar Pradesh-based party, Apna Dal, which won from Mirzapur and Pratapgarh Lok Sabha constituencies in the state. Formed in 1995, Apna Dal is led by Anupriya Patel, daughter of the late Dr Sone Lal Patel, who had been a close associate of the late founder of the BSP, Kanshi Ram. A small party, it nevertheless has some following among the backward classes, and BJP's efforts to forge an alliance with Apna Dal were part of larger efforts to wean the backward castes away from BSP and SP. Shah's preparations were exhaustive: across UP, each page of the electoral roll had a BJP leader in charge. No voter was to be spared.

Secretive and scheming, Shah had been planning various ruses to outwit opponents in Uttar Pradesh when we met him, but didn't share many of his strategies with us. Even so, a couple of hours spent with him were enough to get an idea of his stature in his party. He received numerous calls from Modi, grassroots workers in UP and other BJP leaders. Shah picked up calls to say, "*Bolo* (speak)" and then went into a long listening mode before saying, "*Theek hai* (all right)" and disconnecting the phone. He routinely asked his assistants to make calls to local leaders in our presence. When he spoke to them, he started off saying, "*Dost bol raha hai* (your friend is speaking)."

When Uma Bharti, once a firebrand leader in the BJP, called him ostensibly complaining about dearth of funds and "sabotage" plans by her own party men against her, he told her, "*Didi*, I hope you have a passport. Why don't you travel to the US to propagate Hindu *dharma*? By the time you return, you can take oath as an MP." When she persisted, he added, "Don't you trust your brother? There is nothing to worry and you are winning by a huge margin." Bharti won from the Jhansi constituency by defeating Chandrapal Yadav of the Samajwadi Party and she went on to become Union minister for water resources, river development and Ganga rejuvenation, one of Modi's pet projects.

"He was the one-man army in UP," says a BJP leader from Delhi describing how Shah walked the tightrope of selecting winnable candidates despite earning the displeasure of several senior leaders. He simultaneously went into damage-control mode so as to retain those who were upset about not getting the tickets to contest elections. "The major poll campaigns by the BJP and Team Modi did give the party a lot of advantage. But Amit *bhai* didn't even blink once all through candidate selection, because his mission was to maximise gains for the party here in this crucial state," says a local BJP leader. Shankarbhai Chaudhary, BJP's Gujarat general secretary and MLA from Radhanpura, concurs. Chaudhary has known Shah to be someone who doesn't take 'no' for an answer. "He has always been a doer and therefore we are not surprised by what he did in UP," he notes.

The release of the candidates list in UP was followed by protests, but Shah was seemingly unperturbed. He dismissed all the bickering, saying "longer queues are natural where there is a greater possibility of victory." But that was just posturing, and Shah himself knew it. Chants of disappointment in many parts of the state would have rattled the faint-hearted – some reports pegged troubles in thirty Lok Sabha seats. Former UP Assembly Speaker and BJP leader Kesri Nath Tripathi, an aspirant for the Lok Sabha ticket from Allahabad, had publicly lashed out at party nominee Shyama Charan Gupta, saying that Gupta wasn't even a member of the BJP. The BJP, which had entered into a tie-up with Apna Dal for Mirzapur and Pratapgarh seats, also had to face ire against the nomination of Kirti Vardhan Singh, who had recently joined the party from the SP, in the Gonda Lok Sabha constituency. The party also earned the wrath of a section of local workers over nominating former Congress leader Jagadambika Pal, who had just joined the BJP, from Domeriyaganj. Former state BJP chief Surya Pratap Shahi also voiced his displeasure about not being selected for Deoria in place of BJP hotshot Kalraj Mishra.

Badri Narayan, social historian and cultural anthropologist who is a professor at the GB Pant Social Science Institute, Allahabad, had watched Uttar Pradesh's politics for long. In the run-up to the polls, he had forecast that such whiffs of dissent from various regions would turn a spoiler for the BJP in UP.

They didn't.

***

Most BJP leaders in the state and elsewhere I spoke to give the credit for "silently managing dissent" to Shah. Like the word of comfort he had for an irascible and complaining Bharti, Shah made it a point to meet those 'slighted' leaders and make them feel important. In the first place, he convinced them that the BJP had to make a list of suitable candidates on the basis of caste and other extraneous considerations. "Amit *bhai* not only marvellously managed the caste equation in UP by the choice of the candidates, but he also placated those who didn't get the tickets and enthused them to become very active in the day-to-day aspects of the election campaign," Chauthaiwale avers.

Shah did it with panache. In one instance, BJP leader Shrikant Sharma who was hoping to be a candidate from Mathura had to make way for actor Hema Malini. Sharma, obviously, was extremely upset. A few days later, Shah called him to say, "Shrikant, I am going to Meerut (for the poll campaign). Why don't you join me?" Shah had an intimate chat with Shrikant for three to four hours en route to Meerut, and told him that he was important for the party – and that he needed to plunge into the campaign. From the very next day, the sulking Sharma became very active in campaign duties, having realised that in politics, opportunity strikes unexpectedly. Sharma was recently elected secretary of the BJP, in a reshuffle of the party organisation after Shah took over as president.

A constant troubleshooter, Shah also had to reason with former UP Chief Minister Kalyan Singh – who had returned to the BJP fold recently after aligning with SP in Uttar Pradesh for a while – that he could no longer nurse hopes of fighting the polls. You should take on the role of a mentor of the party while your son Ranveer contests the polls, Shah told him. Singh got the message. The 82-year-old was suitably rewarded after the polls when he was named the governor of Rajasthan.

Never underestimate Shah, forewarns a BJP leader from Gorakhpur. In fact, says he, several months before the 2014 Lok Sabha polls, Shah scouted for bankable candidates with the potential to deliver in a state that had been crucial for BJP's past wins. The challenges were daunting: just two years earlier, in the assembly elections, the rival SP secured a massive 223 seats in the 403-seat House compared with ninety-seven seats it had won five years earlier. Winning them back needed firepower of the highest order.

A few months before the polls, Shah had a list of candidates formidable enough to take on the biggest opponents from SP, the BSP and the Congress. And long before the protests began, he was fully prepared on using carrot-and-stick methods to reign in 'erring' party men, a senior party leader from the state told me.

Shah was also determined to streamline all processes, including allocation of funds. It helped that he knew what exactly was happening everywhere. Because he was in touch with grassroots-level workers, he didn't have to go through mid-level party leaders to have his finger on the pulse of local goings-on. He also had a trusted aide in Akhil Bharatiya Vidhyarti Parishad (ABVP) leader Sunil Bansal. Bansal, who is from Rajasthan, is a master organiser, BJP leaders in the state say. Bansal is like Lakshman or Hanuman to Amit *bhai*, says Chauthaiwale, referring to the two characters in the *Ramayana* who were considered most loyal to Lord Ram. "Without him, Shah would not have done so magnificently in UP. Sunil is absolutely down-to-earth. He did simple things that resulted in a sea change in the way elections were organised. Previous tradition was that if you want to send some money to some candidate, it had to go through a third person (which often meant that that middleman would take his share before he handed it over). Sunil said, 'Nothing doing. Open a bank account with a national bank; we will transfer the money online'. So he effectively ended the brokerage culture, which was very prevalent in UP," he adds. Besides Bansal, Shah had put together a team of canny organisers to assist him in UP, including the likes of Rameshwar Chaurasia, Satyendra Kushwaha, Trivendra Rawat, Captain Abhimanyu, Hridyanath Singh and others.

The BJP may have been a recipient of huge funds from generous donors, but that didn't mean Shah and Bansal did not keep an eye on every little bit of expenditure. Chauthaiwale remembers an instance when the team he was part of came out with a mini booklet on the poll manifesto. Bansal wanted to get him the best deal when it came to printing costs. "My printer had been charging me Rs 2.50 per booklet. Bansal asked me to mail him PDFs so that he could get the booklets printed at Rs 1.50 from someone else," recalls Chauthaiwale, who worked closely with Manoj Ladwa, a London-based mergers-and-acquisitions lawyer, handling the mainstream campaign in TV, print and radio for the BJP besides coordinating with various war rooms and the PM candidate himself.

Rishi Raj Singh, an IIT graduate who volunteered for the BJP during the elections and spent a lot of time in UP during the polls, tells me that one of Shah's biggest strengths was that he had a robust monitoring mechanism, something that corroborates his James Bond-like qualities that his friends admire and detractors abhor.

"When we were actually running the election process, he was firm about how transparent and accountable everything should be. He had very clear objectives in mind and would pose very clear problem statements to us. That's how we too were very purposeful in our approach and our objective – we would go on ground and implement it exactly as planned. And everything was monitored by him. If a particular work had been given to a particular section of the party of a particular district in UP, then every few days, he would follow up to see if the person who was given the responsibilities was actually acting on them," recalls Singh.

The combination of Shah and Bansal was especially fearsome for party workers who had become used to collecting funds on their own.

A BJP functionary recalls how Shah surprised a candidate when the latter demanded money for campaign expenses. Shah already knew from his sources that the candidate was collecting funds on his own from local industrialists and was awash in cash. "Shah just told him, 'Open your cupboard. All the money is there'," the BJP leader quoted Shah as saying. Caught on the wrong foot, the candidate sought redemption and was forgiven with a warning.

The case of Murli Manohar Joshi trying to hold on to the Varanasi seat was dealt with differently, as mentioned in the previous chapter. "Shah could get really blunt at times," says a Delhi-based BJP leader, adding that the attribute has earned him a lot of foes. In Gujarat, many of his ministerial colleagues have complained about his "nasty and rude" demeanour – something that is never couched in sophistication. He has also had a long-standing rivalry with a few comrades, the most notable being the current chief minister of Gujarat, Anandiben Patel, who, like Shah, is a Modi favourite.

Seated before me just after a whirlwind tour in the hinterlands of western UP, Shah readily agrees that his messages are rarely nuanced. "I am blunt," he admits. It's no exaggeration to say Shah is almost always accompanied by controversy, and that includes several instances of hate speeches against non-Hindus during the poll campaign.

***

It is as if Shah has a penchant for courting trouble.

The 50-year-old portly leader, who now receives Z-plus security cover from the government, certainly carries the record of being a tainted politician. His name had cropped up many times in connection with the 2004 Ishrat Jahan encounter case before India's premier investigation agency, the Central Bureau of Investigation (CBI) finally concluded that it had no evidence against Shah in the killing of Jahan,[1] a nineteen-year-old Mumbai resident, and three others, in a fake encounter by officers of the Ahmedabad Police Crime Branch. The BJP claimed that Shah was being zealously targeted by political rivals to bring disrepute to his mentor, Modi.

Shah, an RSS volunteer since childhood and later a leader of the student organisation, ABVP, was then held accountable by the CBI for having orchestrated the killings of Sohrabuddin Sheikh, a criminal, his wife Kauser Bi and an associate, Tulsiram Prajapati. The CBI had alleged that Shah had been paid to do so by some marble traders of Rajasthan who were being harassed by Sheikh for protection money. Shah had gone underground to evade arrest and had stopped using his official mobile phone and his official car as home minister of Gujarat. He was finally arrested on 25 July 2010 and released from jail three months later on bail. In the case, the CBI had charged Shah with murder, extortion and kidnapping besides five other sections of the Indian Penal Code. Shah had to leave Gujarat and stay away till the Supreme Court decided on a CBI plea that his bail be cancelled. In 2012, the top court confirmed bail for Shah and allowed him to return to Gujarat – Shah contested the assembly polls in December and won the elections by a huge margin.

Then, in November 2013, two websites, Gulail.com, and Cobrapost.com, reported that a Bangalore-based woman's phone had been illegally tapped in 2009, reportedly under instructions of Amit Shah and the state police. According to Gulail.com, "Gujarat IPS officer GL Singhal, who is an accused in the Ishrat Jahan fake-encounter case and out on bail, has handed over hundreds of recorded telephonic conversations to the CBI revealing how the three key wings of the Gujarat police – the state intelligence bureau, also known as CID intelligence, the crime branch, and the anti-terrorist squad – misused their powers to stalk an unmarried young woman from Bangalore, whose parents stay in Gujarat."

Shortly thereafter, Pranlal Soni, father of the woman who was allegedly snooped upon, declared that he himself had requested Gujarat Chief Minister Narendra Modi to "look after" his daughter, linking India's current prime minister to the incident. The Congress government at the Centre lost no time in ordering an inquiry commission to probe the alleged snooping on an unmarried woman architect by Gujarat officials reportedly at the behest of Shah. The more vocal of the Congress leaders alleged that Modi was infatuated with the girl and had been stalking her. The BJP denied these claims as preposterous and hit back saying the whole incident was an effort to malign its PM candidate Modi ahead of polls.

***

None of these allegations of vice and avarice for power can however dull Shah's political cunning and his ability to convert adversity into opportunity. His long-time colleagues see Shah, who himself has won polls with record margins, as a grand master in the art of elections.

Shah has contested twenty-eight elections since 1989 to the state assembly and local bodies in Gujarat. He lost none. He fought his first election in 1988 to a primary cooperative body. In 1989, he became president of Ahmedabad District Cooperative Bank, the biggest cooperative bank in the country. Elections to such bodies are usually won on caste considerations. Such banks have traditionally been controlled by Patels, Gaderias and Kshatriyas, and Shah managed to win despite the cooperative sector being a no-go zone for Banias like him.

Shah had been an MLA (member of the Gujarat legislative assembly) from Sarkhej for four straight terms: 1997 (by-poll election), 1998, 2002 and 2007. In the 2002 poll, he had the highest victory margin among all candidates in the state – 1,58,036 votes. In the next election in 2007, he bested his own margin. In 2012, he returned from jail on bail to contest from the Naranpura constituency (following delimitation, Sarkhej ceased to exist).

Shah, the youngest minister in Modi's 2002 Cabinet, had been a multi-tasker in the state government led by Modi, and at one point in the twelve years that Modi was in power, Shah held some twelve key portfolios in the Gujarat government. It is his powers at juggling responsibilities with ease that caught the attention of BJP President Rajnath Singh in 2012 – contrary to popular perception, it was Singh, not Modi, who put Shah in charge of party affairs in UP. Singh was enamoured of Shah's organisational skills in wresting control of various Congress-run enterprises in Gujarat. Shah had led the massive operation of seizing control of local banks, local bodies, including cooperative units and sports bodies. He is now president of the Gujarat Cricket Association.

Eventually, of course, it was Shah's friendship with Modi that catapulted him into the higher echelons of power inside the BJP. After the stunning poll results of 2014, he was declared the president of the BJP.

***

Despite Shah's political successes, his anti-Muslim rhetoric has earned him a bad name. He has also come under sharp attack for instigating communities against each other as part of poll gambits.

As the chief guest at a function held in SDJ high school of Raajhar village, forty kilometres from Muzaffarnagar, Shah made an incendiary speech that was covered in discomfiting detail by Neha Dixit of the news website, Scroll.in. Shah went to the meeting along with the likes of by BJP legislator Suresh Rana, who was imprisoned for twelve days for his role in precipitating riots in Muzaffarnagar and Shamli in August and September 2013, which left sixty-two people dead.

Shah – who did not use a microphone for fear of violating the Election Commission's model code of conduct, which prohibits the use of microphones without permission – was quoted in the report by Dixit as saying, "This is the time to avenge. The leaders standing next to me" – he pointed to Suresh Rana and Hukum Singh (another BJP leader) – "have also been humiliated. A man can sleep hungry but not humiliated. This is the time to take revenge by voting for Modi. This will defeat both the governments: the one at the Centre

and the UP government who lathi-charged and tortured our leaders."
Several accused in the Muzaffarnagar riots – all of them from the Jat
community – were present at the meeting. Wooing Jats in western Uttar Pradesh is crucial in twenty-five
Lok Sabha seats in the state. The Muzaffarnagar riots resulted in
cracks within Hindu and Muslim Jats, and the Hindus began to veer
towards the BJP. Jats in the region have been the traditional vote base
of Ajit Singh's Rashtriya Lok Dal (RLD).

Without doubt, the famed camaraderie between Muslim and
Hindu Jats in the region had come apart following the riots – and
the biggest beneficiary of this divide turned out to be the BJP.

***

Historically, farmer agitations were led by Muslim and Hindu Jats
marching shoulder to shoulder. The late Mahendra Singh Tikait, a
legendary peasant leader from western Uttar Pradesh's Jat belt, used
to count on Muslim faces as an integral part of his agitations. Many
Delhi residents still remember a ten-day siege of Delhi in 1988 where
Jats wearing turbans marched in rhythmic cadence alongside Muslims
in their own traditional headgear. Muley Jats, whose forefathers of
the Jat caste had converted to Islam, enjoyed enormous cultural
affinity with the region's land-owning Hindus. Many of these
'Muslim brothers' were partners in farming and members of Jat-only
wrestling teams. While Jats famously had affection for Muslims in
the region, they looked down upon and even persecuted the Dalits.
Tikait had invited punishment for making derogatory remarks
against former UP chief minister and Dalit leader Mayawati by
referring to her caste.

Once amiable Hindu-Muslim Jat relations in western UP have now
been upset by outbreaks of violence, especially the Muzaffarnagar
riots sparked off by reports of Muslim youths harassing a Dalit girl.
Soon, Jats joined hands with Dalits, resulting in a conflagration. At
least sixty-two people died in the August–September 2013 riots that
wracked the small town. Many more were injured and more than
50,000 displaced. But the veracity of such reports – of a Dalit girl
being sexually harassed – remained highly questionable and many
reports suggest business rivalry between communities as a trigger.

In an interview to me, acclaimed sociologist and author Dipankar Gupta had said before the elections that the political situation in the state following the riots was expected to favour the BJP. "This unsettling of social and political equations in the region (where Muslims account for 26 percent of the population) will play a crucial role in the next polls." He, however, ruled out any significant "warming up" of Jats to Dalits. In fact, the BJP began to attract young Jats following the Ram Janmabhoomi movement.

Gupta elaborates, "Young (Jat) people had started showing interest in the agitation that catapulted the BJP to mainstream politics. By then, the rural economy was evolving fast and old boundaries were quickly losing their sanctity. It was par for the course until the 1970s for Hindu Jats or Muslim Jats to symbolically make fun of each other on the day of Holi. But, by the 1980s, that was no longer allowed, though Muslims and Hindus were still part of the same wrestling team." The only time the BJP made headway in western UP, by securing a chunk of the Jat vote, was after the religious polarisation wrought by the Babri Masjid demolition of 6 December 1992. Even then, only the younger generation of Jats voted for the party. And very soon, they too switched to backing former Prime Minister Charan Singh's son Ajit Singh of Rashtriya Lok Dal as the religious fervour faded over the rest of the 1990s.

Gupta may insist that the Muzaffarnagar riots were not pre-planned, but the method in the madness is inescapable.

SS Gill describes in his book *Islam and the Muslims of India: Exploring History, Faith and Dogma* how misreporting and exploitation of economic rivalry between communities have proved a lethal weapon in the hands of vested interests. According to him, after Gandhi's assassination by Nathuram Godse, there followed a decade of relative calm. "The riots of 1961 in Jabalpur broke this calm," he writes. He quotes a report by a national daily which had sent a reporter there to find out what happened. The story went this way: A Hindu girl was in love with a Muslim boy. The girl committed suicide, no one quite knew why, and the local press falsely reported that she did so because two local Muslim boys raped her.

Gill writes, "The report inflamed communal passions and riots broke out, leaving over fifty dead and many more injured. Two points are noteworthy in this case. First, the local press played a biased role in giving a distorted and inflammatory account of the episode. Second, there was a business rivalry between the father of the Muslim boy – the biggest *bidi* merchant of the region – and an upcoming Hindu adversary, who is alleged to have financed the malicious press campaign... In most of the post-Partition communal riots we find that while the trigger was mostly a local incident, the underlying economic factor provided the muscle."

There are numerous similarities with the riots that have, over the decades, rocked Gujarat, which occupies a prominent place in the history of communal riots in India. Gill says that "Ahmedabad, the centre of a flourishing textile industry, illustrates well the communal tensions that have plagued Gujarat." He finds that "a large proportion of the workforce of Ahmedabad's textile industry consists of Dalit and Muslim workers... A sizeable number of labourers from Uttar Pradesh have also been employed, creating fierce competition for jobs. The riots of 1969 and 1982 were occasioned by the exploitation of economic rivalry between these competing groups by communal elements. Large-scale looting took place during these riots and more than a thousand lives were lost, with the police playing a partisan role." Let's not forget that this was the case before Modi. Later in 2002, months after Modi was elected to power in Gujarat, Gill explains, "Ahmedabad again became the centre of one of the most gruesome, statewide anti-Muslim pogroms and the administration acted in a blatantly biased manner. This was one of the worst instances of religion being yoked to the political wagon."

***

Shah's rabble-rousing didn't end in 'private' functions alone. After being forced to apologise to the Election Commission of India over his comments exhorting Jats to seek revenge, in early May, he did it again – he remarked that Azamgarh, a densely Muslim-populated constituency from where SP leader Mulayam Singh Yadav was contesting, had become a base of terrorists. Shah said, "The accused in the Gujarat bomb blasts were from Azamgarh... Being the then home minister there (Gujarat), I got the accused arrested. Since then not a single terror act has taken place in Gujarat." The poll panel had earlier banned his rallies in UP over his hate remarks.

But then all is well that ends well. After all the theatrics in the big poll game, Shah soon found himself elevated to the league of extraordinary leaders in the BJP. Though the RSS maintained that it was a collective team effort, Modi adjudged Shah the man of the match. Worries about his consistency as a performer may linger, but there were not many claimants to the great victory for the BJP from Uttar Pradesh: seventy-one out of eighty seats and two seats for ally Apna Dal. It was a victory of the scale that shocked Shah himself, he told friends a few days after the emphatic poll win.

Shah has been rewarded handsomely with a plum post – and he is undoubtedly the second most powerful person in the BJP-led alliance. A consummate politician and an inscrutable spinmeister, the new BJP president evokes fear and admiration alike. He is a leader who plays his cards close to his chest to browbeat opponents within and outside his party. He stands by his friends. He is also a down-to-earth householder who derives immense pleasure in spending time with his family – in the months he was banished from Gujarat, he went on a pilgrimage with his wife, travelling second-class by train. Shah isn't one who blinks when faced with the most trying of organisational tangles, yet he sobbed when reports emerged that senior BJP leader Arun Jaitley had lost from the Amritsar seat in Punjab.

Ever since he has taken over as BJP president, Shah is known to work with persistent resistance to any opposition within the party. He is stubborn, unforgiving, determined and wields tremendous power with precision, leaving no option to opponents, even BJP veterans, but to yield. After assuming the top post in the BJP, he initiated an austerity drive within the party, denying the BJP's *pater familias* LK Advani access to the use of chartered planes. Advani is said to have sought an exception, tapping on Shah's doors through another senior leader. Despite close ties with that leader, Shah didn't relent, but merely said, "*Aap yeh baath chodiye* (let's not talk about this)."

He also has no time for whims of allies. The decision to snap ties with 25-year-old ally Shiv Sena in the Maharashtra assembly elections a few months after the win at the Centre was his and his alone. Shah's friends in the party, including Jaitley, were worried. Prime Minister Narendra Modi was about to leave for his crucial, five-day visit to the US when the BJP walked out of the decades-long alliance. Modi, too, was slightly shocked to hear of the news, but finally left it to Shah's discretion. Shah's close comrades were anxious that he was taking too many risks in an election that could be a referendum on his presidency, just as it would be on Modi's prime ministership.

But for Shah, it was more than a political gambit. Shiv Sena, a party formed in Maharashtra in 1966 by political cartoonist Balasaheb Thackeray demanding preferential treatment for Maharashtrians over others, had always been the dominant partner in the alliance with the BJP. Until that moment when he decided to call it quits, Shah's party, despite being a national player, was pulled around like a delinquent by Sena bosses, earlier by the late Thackeray himself and now by his politically naïve son, Uddhav, known for his chauvinistic outbursts. Candidate selections were a one-sided affair. The BJP's list of candidates for the elections was invariably rejected and handed back with a list of the Sena's choices, which were glibly accepted. Senior BJP leaders such as Pramod Mahajan and Gopinath Munde had to suffer the insult with a smile and still cling on to the alliance.

Which is why when Shah decided to snap ties with the Sena, his move was seen as political lunacy or at least a highly risky political proposition. Shah's logic was as simple as his fighting instinct. He disliked the chutzpah of Uddhav, whom he thought arrogant and without substance, unlike his shrewd father. Shah would not take baloney from this man, who issued commands and diktats from Matoshree, the Bandra East, Mumbai, residence of the Thackerays. Shah would wait till Uddhav came to him with a begging bowl. What triggered Shah's move was not just exasperation with the exaggerated sense of importance that Thackeray Junior and his men sauntered around with. He knew that by the time his party parted ways with Shiv Sena, another political divorce would have taken place. The rival, ruling alliance in the state, scarred by corruption and facing the heat of anti-incumbency – of the Sharad Pawar-led Nationalist Congress Party (NCP) and the Congress – was breaking down. That knowledge came in handy.

The Congress would later accuse the BJP of acting in cahoots with the NCP, but then Shah was also driven by the urge to expand his party's base in the state. "If the candidates of our party are decided by our ally, how will we grow *our* party in the state? That was Amit *bhai's* concern," a senior BJP leader told me after the party emerged as the single-largest entity in the state elections held in mid-October 2014. The elections saw a five-cornered contest among the BJP, Congress, Shiv Sena, NCP and Maharashtra Navnirman Sena (MNS). Even though the BJP did not make the clear majority as they did in Haryana, where elections happened simultaneously, and in four other key states where elections took place earlier, they became the only party in twenty-four years to win more than 100 seats from the state, which elects 288 members to the legislative assembly. The highest tally for the BJP in the past was sixty-five in the 1995 elections. Though the 2014 tally of 122 was less than what Shah would have liked, rival parties across India watched in shock and awe.

Shah not only managed to humble the Sena but also helped the BJP spread its wings in the state. Clearly, Uddhav and others were not parleying with the likes of Mahajan and Munde. This was a man whose resolve bordered on the lunatic.

"He could be as ruthless as he could be kind. He is a nice guy," a BJP leader very close to him sums up.

Notes

1. Ishrat Jahan, a college student, was shot dead by police on 15 June 2004 along with three men who had accompanied her at the time. The incident happened near Ahmedabad. The police claimed the group were part of Lashkar-e-Taiba (LeT), a banned Pakistan-based terrorist organisation, and had been involved in a plot to assassinate Narendra Modi. The CBI later said the 'encounter' was fake and carried out jointly by the Gujarat police and the Intelligence Bureau.
2. Pub. Penguin Books India, 2008, New Delhi.

3 | LET THE HYPE BEGIN

"Who says we have to follow a format?"

— Narendra Modi to Piyush Pandey, executive chairman and creative director, Ogilvy & Mather India and South Asia

Overworked, under-slept and probably under-exercised officials at the Election Commission of India (EC) initially enjoyed going through poll commercials made by Modi's campaign team. The videos, with their sense of humour or poignancy, offered them an entertaining diversion from the typical, daily grind of scouring through grievances from political parties, mostly about the words and deeds of rivals. Complaints were many, but they were often routine cases – of vehicles ransacked, workers beaten up, banners burnt, incendiary remarks made against communities and so on. For serious action, one had to wait for weeks until Congress leader Rahul Gandhi went to Solan to warn people that if the BJP was voted to power, 22,000 people would be killed (one wonders how he arrived at that figure?). Or until Modi waltzed into the Amethi Lok Sabha constituency, the Gandhi family's pocket borough, and accused the Nehru dynasty of a "sixty-year-long looting spree".

Their enjoyment of BJP's campaign videos, however, started turning into irritation when members of the party's Election Commission cell, headed by R Ramakrishna, arrived with unfailing regularity every morning, piles of CDs in their arms, requesting the mandatory nod for dozens of TV and radio ads per day. The otherwise amiable EC officials started losing their cool. "Isn't this too much? Do you think we have nothing else to do (other than clearing your scripts)? Go now. Come tomorrow." Finally, when the campaign reached its peak in May 2014, EC officials at Nirvachan Sadan on Delhi's Ashoka Road resorted to expletives: "Fuck, these guys are here again."

In just over two months of April and May, the BJP launched more than 200 major radio ads, as many TV ads, including several twenty-second animated commercials during Indian Premier League (IPL) matches (the popular twenty-over cricket matches known for their glitz and glamour thanks to the presence of peachy-complexioned cheerleaders and Bollywood stars), besides thousands of print advertisements. Almost all commercials were dubbed into more than nine regional languages with local faces and themes.

It was an advertising blitzkrieg unprecedented in Indian polls.

Seated in his expansive, first-floor, almost sea-hugging home in the Mumbai suburb of Mahim, advertising hotshot Piyush Pandey says he can't walk into a party or a meeting these days without being assaulted with questions on his experience of heading the advertising campaign for Narendra Modi in the 2014 polls. "I have said this before and I am saying this again. The war on the field is won thanks to the *karyakartas* (grassroots workers), and the leaders. We just provided the air cover," he laughs as torrential rains lash Mumbai at dusk, obstructing an otherwise grand view from his living room of the Taj Land's End hotel across the bay. He brushes off accolades on his role. "The wave was Modi's. We rode the wave. Yes, we held some fantastic catches, but we did not do the bowling. Yes, we played our role brilliantly but it was only *one* of the roles – we were one of the eleven people in the cricket team. We're happy that the team won; we're happy we came out looking good because our team won. But to believe that the ads are the man of the match? I'm sorry, but Mr Modi was the man of the match from day one, even before the match started," asserts Pandey, who has played professional cricket in the past.

The BJP contract was Pandey's first political campaign and "it was crazy". "Some report said my home, this one, had become a fortress where we were creating commercial after commercial for Modi. It was not out of here that we worked. It was at Taj Vivanta, Delhi, where we had rooms and where we had housed my people," he explains, chain-smoking and massaging his broad moustache as he sips his whiskey and enjoys the rain outside – he instructs his domestic help not to close the balcony windows despite the thunder and sheeting downpour.

Pandey, who collaborated with the Ogilvy and Mather (O&M) agency Soho Square for BJP's poll extravaganza, always loved lightning, thunder and storms. He relished creating them to hard-sell a product.

So why had he always turned down offers to handle political campaigns earlier? It appears there was an issue of tradition at play. David Ogilvy, O&M's founder who is often hailed as the father of advertising, was against the idea of working with politicians. One of the many hazards of working with them, the American ad legend had argued, was not being paid on time besides having to mislead consumers about cantankerous politicos. Those were the same reasons that had held Pandey back in the past.

***

Pandey was introduced to Modi around 2011 by none other than Bollywood's topmost film icon Amitabh Bachchan, who had by then become the brand ambassador for Gujarat tourism. "People ask me how I managed to rope in Mr Bachchan for the Gujarat Tourism ad campaign. And I tell them, it was Mr Bachchan who roped *me* in for this campaign," he chuckles.

Pandey worked with Modi for more than three years, making commercials for Gujarat Tourism, which also entailed spending many hours interacting closely with the chief minister who wielded tremendous influence in all state-government departments and their projects. Pandey discovered early on that Modi was astute and massively knowledgeable, especially when it came to his cherished Gujarat. Before embarking on the tourism campaign, Modi insisted on briefing Pandey's team personally, and Pandey was mightily impressed by the BJP heavyweight's vast knowledge of the history, geography and mythology of various places in the state. "His assistants had given us a time slot of thirty minutes for the briefing, but it took him forty minutes just to talk about one location," Pandey recalls, noting that Modi's education was not the kind based on reading history books, but by exploring places on foot. The Gujarat aficionado could recall populations of districts entirely from memory, even key periods when a change occurred due to natural or political factors, says Pandey.

As soon as Pandey started working on the campaign, he struck up a good friendship with Modi, a rapport based on respect. "At the end of our first day of shooting in Gir, I got a call from Mr Modi. I thought he would ask me how the shoot went. Instead, his first question to me was, 'Are my people taking care of you?' What an amazing way to start a conversation," he marvels, adding, "These are the things of partnership, of conversation-openers. We see these little bits in his speeches, an anecdote here, a touch of humour there. He's phenomenal." It is obvious that Modi had won Pandey over.

But Pandey stuck to the Ogilvy tradition when it came to poll campaigns. He refused an offer from Modi to work in the 2012 assembly elections, arguing that it was not his cup of tea.

2014 was meant to be different. At a meeting in mid-January 2014, Modi called Pandey aside for a couple of minutes, looked him straight in the eye and said, bluntly, "I need your help. This time, don't say no."

A few weeks later, on 2 February 2014, Piyush Goyal, the BJP treasurer, called to confirm the association. "I knew that we were entering uncharted territory, but I didn't want to refuse," Pandey remembers. By then he had discussed the offer with his worldwide CEO who had said, much to his surprise, "Why not?"

When Pandey broke the news to colleagues, there was chaos. Not because they were opposed to the idea of Modi for PM, but because it was an entirely different project, quite unlike anything they had handled before. First, there was not much time. The whole process of signing up for the campaign took a few days, and from 16 February, they were on board in the thick of election fever. "Unlike the Gujarat Tourism project, the deadline here was invariably 'tomorrow'," Pandey says, wryly. Second, Pandey did not go public about his company's role for a while. "There was skepticism on our part," he admits. "We wondered what it would be like working for a political party without a marketing manager – which is what we were used to in our day-to-day work. These were political heavyweights with strong points of view. How much space would we get to express ourselves? Who would be the decision-maker? All these questions came to mind," Pandey recalls.

Meeting BJP leaders such as Arun Jaitley, Amit Shah, Nirmala Sitharaman, Prakash Jadvekar and Piyush Goyal allayed his fears a bit. These appeared to be a sorted-out group of people who were very clear about what they wanted, he thought.

True, those were still days of dilly-dallying over the thrust of the campaign, but it was soon obvious to Pandey and team that this was a presidential-style campaign with the entire focus on Modi because his popularity was, according to an internal survey, much higher than his party's. Initial hiccups over BJP leaders such as Sushma Swaraj and Rajnath Singh apparently insisting on a party-focused campaign died down very shortly.

Making the party's advertisements attractive and meaningful for a larger population was, of course, a vital aspect for the BJP, which had experienced miscalculations in this regard in the past. Exactly ten years earlier, in the 2004 general election, the BJP-led coalition – which was awash in corporate cash – lost out after being in power since 1999, despite a high-voltage campaign titled 'India Shining'. Voters decisively rejected the ruling Hindu nationalist party, confirming fears that India's so-called economic boom during NDA rule did very little to lift the fortunes of the majority. The NDA, which made a serious political misstep by calling the elections six months early, was routed in the first all-electronic elections in the country.

The BJP had hoped that a bountiful monsoon that year, rising growth rates and a reviving peace process with Pakistan would have persuaded voters to give then Prime Minister Atal Bihari Vajpayee another five years in office. Leaders of the BJP-led alliance, especially the late Pramod Mahajan, offered morning interviews while walking on their treadmills and were extremely confident of a victory thanks to all the optics that the campaign blitz had created. The Congress, however, successfully tapped into concerns of the rural poor who were worried that the economic growth benefited only the rich in the cities. In hindsight, the 'India Shining' slogan showed a disregard for the majority, and the Congress and the Leftist parties ended up reaping benefits by highlighting this bias against the poor in both rural and urban areas. The BJP's posturing easily helped its rivals stereotype the party as focused merely on the urban middle class and corporates. Much to their anguish, the BJP later realised that it had completely underestimated its bleak prospects in the two key states of Andhra Pradesh and Tamil Nadu. Besides, many NDA allies who had pulled in minority votes in their states were in dire straits after the anti-Muslim Gujarat riots of 2002. The people of the nation were tired of divisive politics.

By 2014, however, the Congress-led UPA government had lost its sheen and their cadre was disorganised, disgruntled and in total disarray. The ball was once again in BJP's court.

***

The first campaign Soho Square launched was the *Janta maaf nahin karegi* (people won't forgive) series, which featured an individual talking about his or her plight in the face of insurmountable odds such as power shortage, price rise, corruption and so on – issues that BJP placed squarely on the shoulders of the ruling UPA. People were chosen from across the country for regional variants of this ad.

The video advertisements had a grim feel, with the spotlight on one person narrating a back-story. In one ad, for instance, a man narrated how he was forced to give up using his scooter due to rising fuel prices, and switch to public transport. Then food prices went up and he was no longer able to feed his children, which is when he began asking himself, what is going on? The advertisement ended with his vowing not to forgive those who deprived his children of food, and the campaign slogan:

Bahut hui mehengai ki maar / Abki baar Modi sarkar

Chalo haalaat badlein, desh ki sarkaar badlein, Abki baar Modi sarkar

(Enough of battering by inflation / this time, Modi government Let us change our circumstances, let us change our government / this time, Modi government)

Other variations of this advertisement zoomed in on faces of common people, vowing not to forgive a UPA government that had created hurdles and difficulties for them, shot in black and white. The effect was dramatic, the faces serious and angry, the cinematography professional. The last line of each commercial *Abki baar Modi sarkar* – inspired largely from the motto, *Abki bari Atal Bihari* (This time, Atal Bihari) used successfully in the nineties by the BJP for Vajpayee – was lapped up by the public and went on to become the key refrain of the entire election campaign.

If Pandey found BJP leaders like Jaitley and Sitharaman 'sorted out', it didn't mean proposals by Soho Square weren't put to criticism. When the concept was first presented to the BJP team, there was discomfort and skepticism. This was something out of the ordinary, something unheard of for a political campaign. Where were the shenanigans, the old way of storytelling? Instead of narrating a tale, the viewer was being asked to stretch his or her imagination and visualise what may have happened in the past. Instead of overt suggestion, this was a covert emotional appeal disguised as a rational argument.

It was precisely what one would expect from one of the largest and most acclaimed advertising experts in the world.

The argument that minimalist videos, if conceived well, would leave a great impact was valid. After all, the most famous political ad of all time, the "Daisy Girl" ad, which swung public opinion in favour of American presidential candidate Lyndon Johnson in 1964, was a very simple commercial showing a little girl picking petals off a flower – as if in a countdown to a nuclear explosion. This ad implied that Johnson's rival Barry Goldwater was a reckless man; the reaction to the ad at that time was so phenomenal that Goldwater could never shake off the reputation of being an 'extremist' politician.

Despite initial misgivings, it didn't take long for BJP bigwigs to accept Pandey's explanation and approve the campaign. They fell in line with Modi's attitude towards Soho Square, treating the agency as professionals hired for a job they knew best, and not as vendors who had been outsourced for mechanical execution. It was this shift in approach that made all the difference, says Pandey in retrospect.

He observed that a few key people in the BJP core team were true leaders and decision-makers who made his job easier. Once, for instance, current Union minister Nirmala Sitharaman – whom he calls a 'great confidence-giver' – took him aside at a meeting and told him, "You are absolutely right. Stick to your point. Otherwise this meeting can go haywire. I love what you're doing." In another instance, when Pandey presented short animated films to be shown on TV during the IPL matches, she encouraged him in a similar way, "This is brilliant stuff."

In yet another instance, there was a debate over the use of the word *pragati* versus *vikas*, both of which mean progress. Pandey wanted to use the term *pragati* in one of the advertisements, as it is more easily understood by the common man, but some of the party workers wanted to use the word *vikas*, often flouted by politicos. Modi's main man Amit Shah put an end to the discussion, saying curtly, "Cut the crap. The ad-agency people are saying *pragati*, use that. Move on."

"All it takes is two or three key people to say they love it, and then everyone else falls in line. Decisions are made by leaders, not committees," muses Pandey, quoting David Ogilvy, who asked, "Have you ever seen statues of committees in a park?" He is firmly of the opinion that the success of the campaign was due to leaders like Shah, Sitharaman, Piyush Goyal, Arun Jaitley and a few others who took important decisions at crucial moments. "Otherwise these discussions in committees would not end till the cows came home," he laughs heartily.

Contrary to fears and despite minor hiccups, the BJP had in place a highly reasonable team of party workers to vet commercials to make sure that they fit in perfectly with its political vision. A BJP team at its Ashoka Road office in Delhi – led by the likes of UK-based Modi supporter Manoj Ladwa – had the task of endorsing all TV and print commercials along with other slogans to ensure their compatibility with the overall campaign. For example, a lot of attention had to be paid to ensure that each video and poster had the BJP symbol, lotus, on it. Also, each radio ad or brief film had to be region-specific – it wouldn't do to release propaganda material that denounced law and order problems in BJP-ruled states.

There were many others benchmarks, too. "We had to take extreme caution, be alert all the time and give utmost attention to detail. The planning we did at the BJP headquarters – which was monitored by party leaders such as JP Nadda and Jaitley – was quite extraordinary," says Vijay Chauthaiwale who was part of a team of pros based out of the BJP headquarters whose task was to coordinate between war rooms. This team was spearheaded by Ladwa, who, interestingly, was at the forefront of a years-long campaign demanding a visa for Modi in the UK – which Modi got even before he was elected prime minister.

Pandey vouches that Ladwa and his team did a commendable job in choosing the suitability of video, radio and print ads in states and regions. Besides making sure that ads did not inadvertently attack a favourable state government, they ensured that the actors hired for the job had clean backgrounds and had never endorsed a rival party in the past. Every regional advertisement used different actors to make them more authentic to the local populace. The backgrounds of these actors were checked for criminal records and anti-social behaviour. "When you do something of this magnitude, God has to be on your side – because you can slip up anywhere," says Pandey. There were thousands of ways things could go wrong. Someone who professed a clean police record may be exposed as having skeletons in the closet. Or an advertisement meant for one region may accidentally be released in another. That's when an ad team loses momentum. Here, however, Pandey appears dazed as he recalls how smoothly things progressed: "All our people came out clean, no controversy. No mixed up advertisements in regional papers. No nothing. In my three decades of experience, with any kind of coordination with this quantity of work, something *will* go wrong. That's why I said, God has to be on our side. And this time, God was on our side."

***

At the peak of the poll campaign, *Abki baar Modi sarkar* was the most potent slogan and one of the most popular election catchphrases ever in the history of Indian elections. The highly striking Hindi phrase was an instant hit with the man on the street. It went viral on the Internet and the remarkable coherence of the ad campaign perhaps foretold Modi's decisive win. It spawned several (mostly silly) jokes on social media, such as one that went, "Twinkle twinkle little star / *Abki baar Modi sarkar*" and "*Chutney ke bina dhokla hai bekaar* (*dhokla* is tasteless without chutney) / *Abki baar Modi sarkar*". *Dhokla* is, of course, a Gujarati snack.

The immense popularity of the phrase also meant that there were several claimants to the slogan. As the late US President John F. Kennedy said, "Victory has a thousand fathers, but defeat is an orphan."

I once had a conversation with two non-BJP members of Team Modi just before the final phase of elections on 12 May when one of them claimed it was he who came up with the catchline. At that time, many people from the corporate world had invaded Delhi with similar big talk, making it difficult to tell the sacred from the profane. They had sensed an opportunity for political entrepreneurship amid the groundswell of support building up for Modi across the country. One corporate executive and BJP supporter I met at a posh restaurant in south Delhi claimed ownership of the phrase so convincingly that one had to admire his creative skills.

Light, however, dawned after the polls when Pandey came out in an interview saying he was the father of the *Abki baar Modi sarkar* refrain. Until then, he had remained tight-lipped about his involvement in the entire project, often wrought by frustration at being unable to lay claim to something that was becoming bigger and bigger with each passing day. He was also pained to hear his peer Prasoon Joshi, award-winning filmmaker, lyricist and CEO of McCann Worldgroup India, being lauded for working on the BJP campaign, when, Pandey claims, Joshi only created a couple of advertisements – one of which had caused great embarrassment to the party and had to be pulled down within days.

Joshi had also created a full-length song in the initial stages of the election campaign, *Saugandh mujhe iss mitti ki, mein desh nahi mitne doonga* (I vow on the soil of my land that I will not let my land be washed away) which featured Modi's voice punctuating a high-decibel passionate appeal for political change. It was launched at a press conference by Arun Jaitley, who had played a major role in the creation of the song.

Pandey disclosed to the media after Modi's stunning victory that his team – which included thirty people in his agency Soho Square spread across Mumbai and Delhi – came up with 125 artworks across TV, radio or print, every single night within two months. People who assisted him include ad men Anuraag Khandelwal, Satish deSa, Nilesh Jain, Rajkumar Jha and Pawan Bhatt.

While Pandey wrote the hugely popular *Abki baar Modi sarkar* and *Janta maaf nahi karegi* slogans for numerous commercials, Khandelwal wrote the equally powerful *Achche din aanewale hain* (good days are coming) line that continues to be a hit among Modi admirers. Pandey was assisted by the likes of Shoojit Sircar – the National Award-winning director of Bollywood films such as *Vicky Donor* and *Madras Café* – in making close to ten short films every night. Manish Sherawat, an animation expert, made TV spots featuring Modi for broadcast during IPL cricket matches. Sherawat is a product of the National Institute of Design (NID), a premier design school based out of Ahmedabad. "I needed someone who could keep things confidential and who was also highly creative. Manish and I worked as a two-man team – I would write the script and Manish would make the storyboard," Pandey says. In fact, that was an out-of-the-box campaign, and it had to be, Pandey posits. "The audience is very different out there – they were young and they would be high on cricket when these ads were to be broadcast. I couldn't very well do something with a lot of *rona dhona* (crying). I told the BJP guys I wanted to make an animation film. We would use satire; we would be inspired by the cartoonists of the world." Initially, Team BJP were taken aback, but eventually they decided to let the expert do his job and got on with theirs. "I did seventeen of those, they were twenty seconds each. They became a rage overnight," Pandey remembers.

The first of the animation series launched with the line:
Bina captain ke team karegi haar,
Isliye abki baar Modi sarkar.
(Without a captain, the team will lose / That is why, this time, Modi government)

With a bespectacled cricket umpire as protagonist, the cartoons were simply sketched black lines on a saffron background with a cheeky sense of humour that relied on the audience's knowledge of politics to make their point. The first one was a dig at the Congress party's lack of leadership; another showed a cricketer offering the umpire wads of cash, which the umpire refused, hinting at the 'corruption-free' promise of 'Modi sarkar'.

A rewarding commercial made by Pandey that had a huge impact on the ground was one that guides people to press on the lotus symbol on the electronic voting machine. Titled *kamal par button dabao* (press the button next to the lotus flower), it was launched in light of complaints that rivals were using Modi's name to misinform illiterate people that his symbol was the cycle, elephant and so on. One of the videos in the campaign showed a person sitting and pressing a button on and off. Another person says to him, "Why are you pressing the button? There is no electricity." The first person says, "I know that; I am just practising. When I press the lotus button, there will be electricity."

Looking back, Pandey says selling Modi was easy. "He is an ad man's delight. He is a doer as evident from his own rallies in the first part of the campaign. He is a person with tremendous energy – would anyone doubt that? He travelled like a maniac; it was insane to see his schedule. Everywhere he went, he changed scripts to match the audience and circumstances, and then he went and delivered them with the same energy as he'd done in the morning somewhere else. So it was a concentrated effort on a daily basis: there was advertising, there were *karyakartas* on the ground, there were 3D rallies and then there were people on social media doing their bit. It was a mega-strategic affair. I don't think any party has thought of their strategy this well, in India at least," he offers. Despite his reluctance to accept credit for BJP's win, there is no doubt that Pandey's advertisements contributed no less to the creation of the Modi juggernaut than rallies and the hi-tech campaign managed by the likes of social-media supporters, grassroots volunteers, various party panels and the RSS, concede BJP leaders.

All those mega sparks didn't come without a cost, however, and Pandey always insisted on working with world-class production teams. He didn't want to create 'Doordarshan-style' (DD) films, he says, referring to India's government-owned national television looked down upon by media professionals for its shoddy production quality. In the process, Pandey disproved David Ogilvy who had feared that politicians – like crime – don't pay. In the first instance, he had put his foot down and said a short film would cost upwards of Rs 15 lakh, and, to his pleasant surprise, party leaders agreed. "Though they had expected the budget to be around Rs 5 lakh per film, they understood my point. I asked them, do you want a DD kind of film? I can make it for Rs 5 lakh. But I won't put my name to it, because it's not me," he recounts. "Secondly, it wouldn't do them any good either. Did they want to make a film for the sake of making a film or were they making a film that would have an impact and get talked about?" He recalls earlier instances of how Modi would brush aside conformists who wanted to stick to tried-and-tested slogans and themes for the Gujarat Tourism campaign. "Modi's attitude was: 'I have hired an expert. The expert has given me a good reason of how we could be different from others. Who said we have to follow a format?' *That* is the beauty of the man," says Pandey with emphasis.[1]

Pandey was in for more welcome surprises when the BJP team paid up on time.

Having broken the Ogilvy habit of keeping politicians at arm's length, Pandey has now grown comfortable in the role. After the national campaign, he also worked with the BJP for its Maharashtra assembly election campaign, and disagrees that Modi is a 'controversial figure'. In an interview to *Mint* newspaper, he said, rather ambiguously, "Straitjacketing Modi as a controversial figure is a very *nouveau riche* statement on someone who is a grassroots person." Besides, Pandey says, his efforts were only meant to complement the whole drive to sell Modi through rallies, social media and other platforms.

Many slogans and ad lines that the BJP used in its campaign had come from the public, too, sometimes from rank amateurs. For instance, the very attractive song *Log kahte hain, Modi aa raha hai* (people say Modi is coming) was created by a Modi fan named Abeer Vajpayee. The song and videos were his personal initiative. He composed the songs and shot their videos at his own cost and sent them to Modi's team. When Modi came across the videos, he immediately saw the potential in them, and sent them off for distribution across social networks and mainstream media; it was even converted into a caller tune for mobile phones. Besides, there were numerous pro-Modi videos uploaded on YouTube by enthusiasts. The BJP campaign, which had started off on a good note, soon became a powerful bandwagon with various groups chipping in with support, both within and outside India. They included the Patanjali Yoga Peeth of the controversial yoga guru Baba Ramdev, Sri Sri Ravi Shanker's Art of Living, and various independent groups like NaMo Chai Party and so on.

Catchphrases are only as effective as their fulfillment, though. Months after the polls when tangible results of Modi's promises were yet to be realised, the *Achche din aane wale hain* line became a convenient slogan for Modi's detractors to ask: where are the good days?

***

No ad assault or reach-out programme using hi-tech would have made an impact if the party machinery hadn't worked with clockwork precision – the kind they themselves admit had never been attempted before. The BJP set up twenty committees to focus on various aspects of electioneering as early as July 2013 with the intent of campaigning in states such as Madhya Pradesh, Chhattisgarh, Rajasthan, and so on, where local elections were due ahead of the national polls. These twenty teams included a manifesto committee headed by Murli Manohar Joshi and a panel to draft a vision document for the 2014 polls under the leadership of Nitin Gadkari. The campaign committee was led by the likes of senior bigwigs Sushma Swaraj, Amit Shah and Arun Jaitley. Another team led by Shah, former cricketer Navjot Singh Sidhu and Poonam Mahajan set out to woo new voters. There was even a panel led by Rajiv Pratap Rudy, Prakash Javadekar and so on to mobilise intellectuals, and another committee to campaign in the informal sector. To the despair of the Congress, a group headed by the late Gopinath Munde and Ravi Shankar Prasad had specially been set up to highlight the misrule of the UPA. There was also a committee led by Piyush Goyal to handle social media, and another core committee for media, besides an Election Commission cell led by R Ramakrishna.

One of the important teams was a logistics panel headed by Mukhtar Abbas Naqvi, whose job was to arrange helicopters, supply propaganda material such as banners and posters, decide on rally locations, and so on. They were assisted by the 'publication panel' that dispatched booklets, brochures, images, audios, and so on. The information-technology cell was managed by techie Arvind Gupta, an alumnus of IIT and a PhD from the University of Illinois in the US. His team – housed inside the BJP's party office in Delhi's Ashoka Road – disseminated Modi's messages through mobile phones and social media sites. According to a party insider, the IT cell also helped with research, response to political developments and in generating content.

The amount of cohesion between committee war rooms was massive, rigorous and unparalleled. A person who worked in the Congress's digital war room based out of 15 Gurdwara Rakabganj Road in Delhi says his team was far outnumbered by the BJP's various teams as well as Internet trolls[2] whose movements and responses were guided by the party.

The biggest example of such synergy between data gatherers and those weathering the dust and grime of political campaign was that after receiving booth-wise data on performance by the BJP, the RSS and the party placed ten people each at 3.5 lakh of nearly six lakh polling booths in the country. Of these ten, three people were armed with phone numbers and connected to the party headquarters. Any message could be given through SMS or even bulk SMS. This part of the logistics was handled by Arvind Gupta; it was a monumental exercise that helped give instructions and take feedback from the furthest outposts, and was useful in alerting authorities if rival parties created trouble.

Election 2014 proved that several such individual steps were as good as a giant leap. Pundits expect the role of pros in polls to be much higher in India in the future. The trend of hiring political gurus has caught on in parliamentary democracies across the world, with elections now being fought presidential-style even in countries like the UK, which, like India, is a parliamentary democracy. Interestingly, David Axelrod, Barack Obama's most influential adviser during his two presidential victories, has been hired to advise the UK's Labour Party on its 2015 election campaign, to help opposition leader Ed Miliband secure a dashing win and become UK's next prime minister in the May elections.

When the BJP secured 282 seats out of 543 (ten more than required for a simple majority) in the 2014 elections, it was the first time since 1984 that a single party had a majority on its own to run the government without assistance of any allies. BJP was clearly the party of the moment. Its triumph came from hitching its wagon to a star stallion and promoting him aggressively as the messiah India was waiting for.

The gambit paid off.

Notes

1. No official figures for the ad campaign budget have been released though speculation pegged it at anywhere from Rs 400 crore to Rs 10,000 crore. Just ahead of the polls, when I asked then BJP treasurer Piyush Goyal whether the party's advertising budget was upwards of Rs 400 crore, he had said, "If I had 400 crores, then I would be king."
2. In computing jargon, a troll is "a person who submits deliberately inflammatory articles to an Internet discussion".

4 | WAR ROOM

"The word 'right' should be excluded from political language, as the word 'cause' from the language of philosophy."

– Auguste Comte

Efforts to create a Modi wave, or a Modi tsunami, had begun many months before the 2014 polls, in right earnest, in various pockets of India where ordinary citizens unaffiliated to political parties got together to create awareness about their choice of candidate. It helped that most of these self-motivated people were pro-Modi. It further helped that the BJP caught on early to the favourable tendencies of these people and began to cooperate with them to spread the 'M' word.

Inside a government office on Gandhinagar's Infocity campus where a group of young, highly educated graduates from some of India's most reputed institutes was working 24x7 for the nation's cause, I spoke to four of them who had quit high-paying jobs to support the 2014 election campaign. They were glad they were part of the making of history – even a cynic would have been inspired to hear them speak.

Former Credit Suisse executive Rishi Raj Singh had spent several tough weeks in Uttar Pradesh during the campaign. Born in Kanpur, UP, this affable young man is a chemical engineering graduate of the 2011 batch from IIT Kanpur. Agra-born Gaurav Bhatele, a natural leader capable of long silences and short spells of quick, intelligent chat, is a BTech in aerospace engineering and a former associate with Boston Consulting Group. Like Singh, he, too, passed out of IIT Kanpur the same year. So did the effusive Piyush Jalan, born in Varanasi, a former business analyst at Deloitte Consulting and a BTech in biological sciences and bioengineering. The superbly confident and creative Nandan Jha, seated towards my left, is two years younger than the rest: a native of Dharbanga, Bihar, he graduated from IIT Bombay in 2013.

"We were not very happy with what we were doing in our corporate jobs. We wanted to do something more. So we came together," starts off Bhatele, who – along with his friends – is a member of what has now attained a cult status among election managers, a group named Citizens for Accountable Governance (CAG). It is a not-for-profit NGO launched by Modi's Man Friday and former UN health official, 35-year-old Prashant Kishor. Any resemblance to the other CAG (Comptroller and Auditor General of India), the feared internal auditor of the country – which had over the past several years put the government on its toes over several decisions, especially with regard to allocation of air waves and natural resources that it argued resulted in losses amounting to trillions of rupees – is accidental.

Or, considering how the 'Modi wave' took shape, perhaps not.

The world over, frustration among the youth has given birth to various movements, and in free India we have seen young graduates and students adding glamour and gravitas to the Naxalbari movement of the late 1960s, the Poorna Swaraj movement led by the redoubtable Jayaprakash Narayan in the 1970s, and even the Ram temple movement that saw the rise of the BJP as a formidable electoral force. In recent times, student angst and youth anger have eventually gone astray, be it in the Arab world or elsewhere. The Arab Spring – the wave of revolutions that deposed rulers from Egypt to Sudan and continues to lead to violent protests across the Middle East from Syria to Israel, Western Sahara to Palestine and beyond – was one such manifestation of what motivated young men and women could do. In countries such as Greece, which are battling serious economic crises, despair, anger and, sometimes, wounded pride have pushed many young people to throw their lot behind far-

Right political outfits such as Golden Dawn, which is fiercely anti-Semitic and popular. In France you have greater support from young people now for the far-Right National Front led by Marine Le Pen than ever before. Nationalist parties across Europe, from Denmark to UK and Austria, have also gained ground lately.

At CAG, around the time of pre-elections in 2013-14, angry educated Indian youth found a rather more productive outlet.

When they first came together in the summer of 2013, their motley group wasn't yet CAG and they had no inkling that they would run key parts of the Modi campaign. They just wanted to do something very different from their drab corporate work and to help drive growth and development in the country. By the time CAG was formed in mid-2013 out of a group that swelled from ten to thirty to fifty and now 150 permanent members, these young people were busy organising outreach programmes for the youth and first-time entrepreneurs. Their first major event was a 'young India' conference held in June 2013 where they invited some fifty business leaders to discuss their vision for India for the year 2020. Former President Abdul Kalam attended the meet. Narendra Modi also turned up.

Many of them were first-time voters. Their watershed moment – following some unexpected turns of events that meant these young men and women with hardly any experience in political campaigns would become part of the largest democratic experiment ever in modern history – was yet to come.

***

The second event they organised – this time as CAG – was Manthan, in September 2013. The aim of this project was to involve the youth of the country in shaping the agenda of Election 2014. Online participants were asked to provide solutions to fourteen key challenges the country faced in various spheres of life – education, health, livelihood, urban planning and so on. More than 20,000 entries came in from 700 different colleges across 300 cities, says a CAG member. During this campaign, the outreach team of CAG – they had 500 campus ambassadors by then – visited different colleges and told them that the whole competition was meant for connecting the youth with the nation's decision-makers. Shortlisted teams – those who gave the best solutions to some of the vexing problems plaguing India – got a chance to attend the finale at Thyagaraj Stadium, New Delhi, on 2 October 2013, Mahatma Gandhi's 144th birth anniversary. The winners of the competition also got a chance to intern with renowned policymakers from domains such as politics, business and social services. They would further get an opportunity to present their recommendations before leaders from the BJP and the Congress. In all, around five lakh people participated in the entire activity. CAG's website would get over two lakh visitors a day around then.

Manthan gave what the CAG later discovered was a clear edge after it joined Modi's campaign team: a bankable network among a phenomenally large – and fast-growing – group of educated, aspiring young people across the country. During Manthan, CAG conducted a voting among the core team and its associates to assess the country's most popular leader: it was Modi. That was in October 2013. "So we said okay, let's go and support Modi in this election," says Bhatele.

That, in hindsight, was a foregone conclusion.

The reason being that Prashant Kishor, who was befriended by Modi in London when the latter was on a visit to the British capital, before he started working for the Gujarat chief minister in 2011, had sought out these young people and built team CAG with the purpose of creating a backbone for the Modi campaign of 2014. The 35-year-old's aim, after having learnt lessons from the state assembly elections in Gujarat in 2012, was to set up a team that could replace whom he derogatively refers to as 'vendors' – consultants, event managers and their ilk – with an in-house team of committed pros and volunteers who worked in tandem with the BJP leadership. "I firmly believe that to do a presidential campaign, you need your own resources to conceptualise, plan and implement in a preferred manner – you can't rely on outside vendors to do it for you," he told me, stressing that hiring multiple outside agencies for planning and execution of a political party's campaign often proved disastrous and cumbersome. "Which is why I created CAG," he said.

With the success of Manthan, Kishor had a potent youth force that was functional, independent of the BJP and readily swelling. And at the core of the not-for-profit organisation, which first gathered informally in the first week of May 2013 registered under Section 25 of the Companies Act, were graduates from IIM, IIT, Indian School of Business, Stanford, Cornell and so on, who had earlier worked at firms such as AT Kearney, JP Morgan, Michelin India, IBM, Barclays Capital, Merrill Lynch, Deutsche Bank, McKinsey and Company, and Goldman Sachs. They were zealously ready to go for the kill.

Kishor had no doubts whatsoever: it was going to be a presidential-style campaign and that called for selling Modi as aggressively and fiercely as a brand to as many people as possible in a short time, thrust in their minds the image of a no-nonsense leader who could lift the country out of a decade of lethargy, misgovernance and apathy. CAG was ready to go to any extent to do it. Truth didn't matter, hype shall reign.

At the height of the election campaign, Kishor had 400-500 members and ninety-five lakh volunteers working for him at CAG.

***

The promotional ploy around Modi had acquired a professional hue when, in 2009, Modi hired American public-relations firm APCO Worldwide for its Vibrant Gujarat Summit, a biennial function whose purpose was to attract more investment into the state. But Kishor's task was to sustain it and find inventive ways to help Modi strike a chord with the majority rattled by the economic downturn, inflation, and numerous other woes of daily life. "If a person thought, 'Who can be my saviour to lift me out of poverty?', then Modi's face must appear in his mind. That was what we were about to do," says a senior CAG member.

It was going to be no easy task. Battered by accusations that he stood silent as Hindu zealots went on a rampage of destruction and killing after a train carrying pilgrims was burnt at a railway station on 27 February 2002 in Muslim-dominated Godhra, claiming many lives, Modi and his team needed an image overhaul. The US had revoked his visa over the Godhra issue and he became Public Enemy Number One for the media. Efforts to warm up to senior editors

– such as those in *The Times of India* – backfired. Modi had to either walk out of TV studios or request that cameras be switched off when he faced embarrassing questions over the 2002 Gujarat riots – a case in which he was exonerated thrice by courts later. Modi's name was mud in international intellectual and diplomatic circles as well, with the probable exception of a few countries such as Japan and China. Renowned philosopher and Chicago University professor Martha C. Nussbaum told me in an interview after Modi's 2012 victory, his third as Gujarat chief minister, that his triumph was a blot on the people of Gujarat who chose to "re-elect an outlaw". Nobel Prize-winning economist Amartya Sen said in the run-up to the 2014 polls that he disliked the idea of Modi, with his huge divisive appeal, becoming the prime minister of India.

Of course, Modi wasn't sitting idle, letting abuses pass. He had hired APCO to handle the showpiece Vibrant Gujarat Summit. A master of spin, Modi laid the red carpet to welcome corporates to Gujarat. The Tata Group, which was going through pretty bad times in West Bengal where a massive agitation forced the salt-to-car conglomerate to shut its automobile-making units, was promptly offered land in Gujarat to relocate its factories. According to a former APCO official, Modi received a reluctant Ratan Tata, the then chairman of the Group who had earlier looked down upon Modi as a far-Right nationalist, at the Ahmedabad airport and offered him all help. Their ties drastically improved.

Modi even found admirers among academics in American universities. None other than globalisation buff, Columbia University professor Jagdish Bhagwati, in association with colleague and economist Arvind Panagariya, wrote a book in 2012 called *India's Tryst with Destiny: Debunking Myths that Undermine Progress and Addressing New Challenges*,[1] lapping up Modi's Gujarat model of development. The duo argued that the growth-focused economic initiatives by Modi would soon start showing results in the state's otherwise poor social-development index. They went on to challenge Nobel laureate Amartya Sen, saying that it was the "Gujarat model", or growth-focus initiatives, that had delivered results in the southern Indian state of Kerala, and not welfare schemes, as suggested earlier by

Sen. Sen countered with statistics, but by then an impression had been created that Modi was the leader to emulate, and that he was the hope of India.

APCO also got many globally acclaimed journalists and writers such as Robert D. Kaplan and others to interview Modi as part of a massive bid to effect an overhaul of Modi's riots-tainted image. It worked. Professors Panagariya and Bhagwati who told me in early 2013 that they favoured Modi's economics, suggesting that they were yet to endorse his brand of politics, revealed by the end of 2013 that there was nothing wrong with the politics of a man cleared by the courts.

By the time CAG began to support the Modi campaign, it didn't have the burden of having to hold forth on the Gujarati leader's innocence over the riots – instead, having been exonerated by courts, Modi and his team had begun to talk of a witch-hunt by the Congress-led coalition using the federal probe agency. Neither did the CAG team have to peddle what Panagariya had to do in the face of stunning statistics of Gujarat's underdevelopment. By late 2013, it looked like Modi had already bridged the trust deficit with a majority of the people looking up to him as the saviour.

Kishor and his team were now left to magnify that image – and they did it with rigour, enthusiasm and single-minded focus over the next few months, ahead of the polls. There was much hard work and imagination at play, Kishor said. "I had young guys literally falling unconscious in my office," he told me. CAG's top priority was to activate its team of volunteers and come up with innovative ways of connecting with people through them. In each parliamentary constituency, there were one or two CAG members working closely with RSS-BJP leaders, and they were assisted by scores of volunteers who kept enrolling from these regions. Across Uttar Pradesh, for example, there were over eighty CAG members present across its eighty constituencies. In hot-seat Varanasi alone, CAG stationed nine of its core members and some 150 full-time volunteers.

CAG vigorously tapped the volunteer base it had created during events such as Manthan and, later, through the Statue of Unity Movement (SOUM). This latter was an ambitious populist project launched by the Gujarat government in 2010 to build a 184-metre tall statue of freedom fighter and India's first Home Minister Sardar Vallabhbhai Patel (1875-1950), by collecting soil and metal from every nook and corner of the country. Patel is revered by Hindu nationalists like Modi for his tough stance against Pakistan in the early days of Independence – it's an altogether different matter that Patel, the 'Iron Man of India', was never fond of Hindu nationalists in his lifetime and had vehemently criticised the RSS and other Hindu organisations for creating the conditions that led to the assassination of Mahatma Gandhi in 1948.

Soon after they became a bonafide organisation, CAG began handling what was called the "social mobilisation" mandate for SOUM through online and offline activities. It helped dispatch resource kits in which metal (for the statue) was to be collected from different villages around the country. "We dispatched three lakh kits, one to each gram panchayat in the country. It was a major logistical exercise," says a CAG member.

CAG also helped conceptualise and organise a related Gujarat government-run project, Run for Unity. Again held in honour of Sardar Patel who had united 565 princely states to form the Indian Union, the event was held on his death anniversary, 14 December 2013, across 1,100 locations in the country, including remote locales such as Kargil and Leh. The marathons had an unmistakable saffron hue, with BJP leaders making speeches and flagging off the event in different cities. The run in Vadodara was flagged off by Modi; in Ahmedabad by LK Advani and in Delhi by Rajnath Singh, prompting Janata Dal (United) leader KC Tyagi to comment to NDTV, "This is a run for PM's post, not for unity." Exceeding their target of thirty lakh runners, the event eventually found participation of around forty-five lakh people in total. CAG learnt on the job, expanding its network of volunteers.

Digital campaigns projecting Modi as the prime ministerial candidate of the BJP had started more than a year earlier thanks to various groups across social media platforms and other online avenues. When CAG chipped in with campaign support, it immediately created 316 Facebook (FB) pages for various Lok Sabha constituencies for people in those locations to discuss the merits of the BJP's candidates. Of these, 160 were given higher priority because a 2013 Iris Business Services report had identified 160 seats that were higher-impact constituencies in terms of influence potential on the digital population, or the population typically present on FB, Twitter and so on. CAG also used these FB pages to connect with its volunteers across these higher-impact constituencies, such as Thane, Jaipur, Indore, Madurai and Patiala.

***

It was then that fate presented a stunning opportunity. It came in the form of an insult.

At an All India Congress Committee meeting in January 2014, senior Congress leader Mani Shankar Aiyar made a preposterous comment on Modi – that the BJP leader would never become the prime minister but could sell tea at an AICC meet. In the same month, Samajwadi Party's Naresh Agarwal acerbically hinted that a person who once sold tea could not have a national perspective. Agarwal said: "If you make a constable the superintendent of police, he can never have a superintendent's approach but will only have that of a constable," referring to Modi's prime ministerial ambitions.

Simultaneously, the CAG team found itself badgered by its Facebook supporters on the 316 pages they had created. They wished to speak to Mr Modi himself, the volunteers said. They had a lot to talk to him about. Could a conference call be held for all of them? A Google Hangout, perhaps?

The BJP team swung to action mode to develop a plan that could not only attract attention to Modi's poverty-stricken childhood – of having helped his father sell tea in his hometown of Vadnagar in Gujarat – but also connect with the hoi polloi to create the picture of him as a politician engaged in an unrelenting battle against poor governance. "Narendra *bhai* has an enormous political acumen," Vijay Chauthaiwale told me later. "He knows how to convert a small opportunity into a big one."

And so, the now legendary Chai pe Charcha campaign (chat over tea) was launched as an effort at ensuring poetic justice and to counter the insinuations by the rival politicians. Common Indian folk would get an opportunity to chat directly with Modi and convey their problems through video conferencing across thousands of street-side tea stalls all over India – from the metros to the villages and everywhere in between. It was BJP's *coup de main*.

But people like Kishor and others at CAG as well as the BJP leadership realised that while Chai pe Charcha was a grand concept, a trump card of sorts in politics, it would be extremely tough to execute. CAG members were soon on their toes coordinating with multiple volunteers and working in tandem with the Sangh Parivar to make the event a success. For these young former corporate execs, Chai pe Charcha was the on-the-ground version of Google Hangout, and it was an exercise in exactitude. "If I say we worked really hard, that would be an understatement," says a CAG member drily. The first event was to be held on 12 February 2014.

At Chai pe Charcha, to be transmitted to multiple locations – all tea stalls – through video conferencing, Modi would address people gathered at tea-stalls at 1,500 select locations and later answer their questions and listen to their grievances. The timing of these 'debates' was important, poll managers felt. Following consultations with BJP bigwigs, it was decided that Chai pe Charcha would be organised between 6 p.m. and 8 p.m., typically the time when ordinary folk returned from work. The theme for the first round was 'good governance'. All through his years in power as chief minister of Gujarat, Modi had meticulously cultivated the image of a ruler with a distinguished record though the true picture was not completely revealed, as growth figures and other statistics about Gujarat amply indicate. The proceedings of the programme were to be instantly translated into local languages in non-Hindi speaking states. In fact, a precursor to this campaign was launched by the BJP's Karnataka unit, which had set up tea stalls in Bangalore where senior party leaders like former BJP President N Venkaiah Naidu had distributed tea to the public.

Identifying and setting up Chai pe Charcha tea stalls across India was a massive war effort in itself. In the first round BJP workers, used to old bow-and-arrow methods, weren't involved much in the programme – which meant CAG managed Chai pe Charcha on its own with assistance from its volunteer base – lakhs of whom had approached them through local BJP party offices or through online and offline media. The logistics were supplied by the Gandhinagar-based team. Locations were zeroed in among the countryside, urban and "rurban" (semi-urban) areas to cover all social and economic groups. The CAG team asked its volunteers in thousands of locations to identify three tea stalls in their city that were most popular.

As proof that the tea vendor was also ready to work with CAG, the volunteers (three for each location) were asked to shoot a video and send it to the head team; these videos were uploaded on the CAG website. In Varanasi's Assi Ghat, for instance, forty tea stalls, including the famous tea shop Pappu Chai Wala, were covered.

CAG had a central team monitoring the event from Gandhinagar and they were assisted by thirteen different teams from the states. "Any project that was designed here (in Gandhinagar) was to be communicated to the state heads. It was the responsibility of the state head to take care of that particular project in that particular state," a CAG member explains. The head campaign team sent TV screens, publicity posters and other paraphernalia to the volunteers through a point of contact in each state. These volunteers were entrusted with the job of coordination with local residents. "They had to mobilise people and get people to that venue. CAG would do the setup and the volunteers were there to coordinate the audience," the CAG member goes on, explaining that all this was happening at a volunteer level and no one needed to be paid for their efforts. "The Facebook volunteers were extremely motivated; they had been running the pages for a very long time and they had finally got an opportunity to see some real-life action."

Planning and timing was accurate to the T. Volunteers visited the tea stall seven days prior to the event, with a list of ten mandatory items on their checklist, including a recce of the place to check for DTH signals, Internet connectivity, two-way connectivity, availability of generators and so on. Otherwise, buffer locations were to be identified. Permissions had to be taken from local authorities for conducting the event, and vendors hired – these included a man to run the generator and another to set up the DTH connection. Dry runs were held three days prior to the event. "There was a time when I used to make seventy or eighty calls a day just to coordinate with the field teams. The details sent to each and every volunteer were very elaborate. Without such meticulous planning, the programme wouldn't have been a success," says one of the CAG members in the Gandhinagar office.

The team also had to be prepared for the worst, including power cuts and load shedding hours, he adds. Rival governments, such as the Samajwadi Party in Uttar Pradesh, would impose Section 144 (the penal code against "joining unlawful assembly armed with deadly weapon") in an area, disallowing the event. In several other states, hooligans would snatch TV sets away. In some places, tea vendors were beaten up and chased away, and locations had to be changed at the very last minute. In some towns, CAG volunteers were even arrested and their TVs confiscated. CAG had to be on its toes all through. "In our very first meeting with Mr Modi, he had said, 'If you plan for 1,500 and you do 1,499 well and there is a mistake in just one, people will point out to precisely that one.' It was a big, big task for us that maximum locations should go off well," a CAG member says earnestly.

On the day of the event, CAG members went down to the call centre at 7 a.m. and began making calls to all the volunteers around the country to wake up. "Get up; it's Chai pe Charcha today," they said, from their war room. "You need to reach your location by 9 a.m."

Another call went out at 10 a.m.: "Have all the vendors reached the location? Have you started work?"

Another one at 1 p.m.: "Is your TV working? What is in your feed? Can you read out the number we are beaming right now?"

Finally, at 5:30 p.m.: "Has the feed started?" If the answer was yes, the location was confirmed live.

Problems were simultaneously being solved by the boys in the war room. "Sometimes, we were told all three volunteers were not picking up the phone. We would then call the tea vendor and tell him, 'Now you have to organise it yourself'," they chuckle in recall.

At 5:30 p.m. on 12 February 2014, minutes before the first round of Chai pe Charcha was to start, Modi sat in front of a tea stall opposite Karnavati Club on SG highway in Ahmedabad, looking serenely into the wall of television screens in front of him. That's when the first snag struck. The trial video feed didn't work, and so the video could not be transmitted to the central unit in Delhi, which was coordinating with all the other locations. Fortunately, the connections came through a few moments before the show began. But there was still a lag – people asking Modi questions would hear their voice echo after fifteen or twenty seconds. "It appeared as if there were many gaps of silence from both ends," recalls a CAG member.

Despite the hazards and the technical issues, they had managed to 'crack' 95 percent of the target locations, reaching out to forty-five lakh people. "Never before have I sold as many cups of tea as I sold today," a tea vendor in Patna, Bihar, cheerfully told a reporter from *The Hindustan Times*. At some locations in UP and Bihar where power cuts were rampant, the fact that Chai pe Charcha was still live with the help of generators while the rest of the town was in darkness left a deep impression on the sweating crowd. "It was quite symbolic," laughs a CAG insider.

The event had dealt plenty of lessons to the enterprising CAG team, and in the next two rounds, things improved drastically. The time lag in the feed was reduced to five seconds. And instead of CAG having to seek volunteers, they were thronged with offers and requests, and had to shortlist the best of the lot.

The second Chai pe Charcha was slated for Women's Day, 8 March, and the theme, not surprisingly, was 'Women Empowerment'. From this round onwards, CAG enlisted BJP's backing to increase the reach of the event. "We asked the party leaders, for example, which are the five best places in this city for us that are politically relevant as well? They could help us in mobilising people much better than our volunteers could individually do. And so, the party started helping us in the second and third rounds," says a senior CAG member. The third round focused on 'farmer suicides' and targeted rural areas. No location was repeated, and no tea stall was repeated either. In all, Chai pe Charcha covered 4,500 locations, reaching out to crores of people, directly or indirectly.

The campaign added to the Modi mystique – here was a leader who knew about the problems of the common man, one who was ready to discuss them and suggest solutions. It gave people – jaded by the sight of inaccessible leaders touring the streets in their SUVs and official car-cades – an impression that with Modi in power, access to the PM would be easier. Grassroots party men who worked closely on the Chai pe Charcha project note that it had widespread appeal, something they had never expected. First, it was perceived as the complete opposite of a rally where a leader stood on a stage, spoke, and went off. "In this concept, the leader is coming straight to you, to a TV monitor in your city, at a tea stall where you normally hang out. There he wanted to listen to *you* rather than giving a speech. It was like he was in your home," avers a BJP leader from Uttar Pradesh, adding that it was the interactive nature of the programme that made all the difference.

Without doubt, Chai pe Charcha really set the tone, catapulting Modi as a tireless campaigner for his party and the most watched face in the 2014 election. Without doubt, the programme was the trailer to the actual action. Its success also showed the BJP's poll managers, used to traditional ways of canvassing votes, how election campaigning could be done in inventive ways and how the rules of the game could be swung in its favour.

"This programme beamed across to various locations in the country with people speaking different languages but discussing common questions related to farmers, the poor, and so on, struck a chord with the common man. Suddenly, there was this feeling that the next ruler of the country would discuss common people's concerns with them and listen to what they had to say. This was a far cry from the usual mode of campaign where the leader would speak from a distance and go," says a Delhi-based senior Congress leader, ruing that BJP outshone his own campaigners by leaps and bounds.

***

Indeed, in contrast, the Congress' campaign machinery was hobbled by ego clashes among its senior leaders. Innovative campaign suggestions from the Congress war room that operated out of a modest home at Delhi's 15 Gurdwara Rakabganj Road and the 12 Tughlak Lane residence-cum-office of Rahul Gandhi – both of which had the blessings of the Gandhi scion and Congress vice-president – had been brusquely overruled by the Congress headquarters. The clash between the Congress HQ and the war room conceived by Rahul took a heavy toll on the Congress' national campaign. "Their left hand didn't know what their right hand was doing," one BJP leader told me, chuckling gleefully.

Though the Sonia Gandhi-led party had hired PR firm Genesis Burson-Marsteller and Japanese ad agency Dentsu to brush up the Gandhi scion's image and work in rhythm with the members of the war room, which was sponsored by Haryana chief minister and Congress leader Bhupinder Hooda and led by a former journalist, coordination was often off-key to say the least. Though the war room suggested a change of tack – from focusing on the 'achievements' of a scam-tainted Manmohan Singh government to a 'relatively young face' of Rahul – efforts to reach out to people didn't click to a great extent due to discordant notes within the party. There was also an overall failure that came from a 'reluctant politician' like Rahul being pitted against the likes of Modi and Aam Aadmi Party's Arvind Kejriwal, who had been pitched as outliers or agents of change.

The momentum of the Congress campaign had also been hit badly following Rahul's late-January televised interview with senior news anchor Arnab Goswami on Times Now,[2] which was a disaster. Following that, Congress campaign heads began putting up video clips of the 43-year-old leader interacting with small groups – something he was more comfortable with. The brief to the Congress' PR agencies was to focus on Rahul and his emphasis on giving voice to various disadvantaged groups, opportunities to them, transparency in doing things, and how he wanted to empower them. The acronym for all that was 'VOTE'. But the Congress poll push was lassoed by lack of cooperation from various states.

Since Modi's team had transformed the poll fight into a presidential-type campaign, Congress slogans such as "*Mein Nahin, Hum* (Not me, but us)" didn't click. The public had begun to enjoy the NaMo versus RaGa fight (popular acronyms for Narendra Modi versus Rahul Gandhi), and were itching for ring-side views. Political pundits state that Rahul was perceived to be running away from facing Modi, who aggressively targeted the Congress vice-president in each of his speeches, calling him a *shehzaada* (prince). Even a Congress campaign that got over 700,000 hits on YouTube alone – featuring Hasiba B Amin, Goa unit president of the Congress' students wing, National Student Union of India (NSUI), shouting the slogan, "*Kattar Soch Nahin, Yuva Josh* (Not a fanatic mindset, but youthful passion)" – did not make expected impact, says a Congress leader. "Because it was meant to spite Modi at a time when all the 'youthful passion' was in favour of Modi," he reasons. On the contrary, it spawned several spoofs with Gandhi presented as a spoilt young boy and the Congress as a 'fake' party where no one worked.

The Congress also appeared laggard on the Internet side of its campaign thanks especially to the number, tenacity and aggression of Modi fans – these were thousands of individuals who turned up to back the BJP online. Among them were moderates and ultra nationalists and trolls. Moderate ones ran platforms like Centre Right India (CRI), where participants engaged in subtle campaigns to push a centre-Right agenda, discussing issues with remarkable fairness – at least as much as can be expected of the centre-Right – and respect for divergent views. They offered nuanced arguments on a range of topics. Then there was IBTL, short for India Behind The Lens, which churned out clever yet misleading articles and diatribes against political opponents. Its catchy headlines were sheer propaganda, reminiscent of those run by the Communist mouthpieces of erstwhile East Germany. Just when it appeared that Kejriwal would be a force to reckon with, at least in Delhi, IBTL resorted to write-ups bordering on the frivolous. Some of them had headlines such as "Arvind Kejriwal took money and left Anna on his own" and "Twenty-five questions to Arvind Kejriwal and his fan boys", clear attempts at spreading malicious rumours.

Piyush Goyal, then BJP treasurer and now Union minister, had conceded to me in the run-up to the election that the BJP had a lot of loyalists – techies and other professionals he did not identify –

who worked without pay to campaign for the party's PM aspirant. In fact, the BJP had in place teams that worked as command and control centres for trolls who were thrown instructions every time a Rahul speech or a Sonia remark started trending. "That was, I believe, demoralising for the Congress campaign. But then, the Modi campaign always had an upper hand, and was like a well-oiled machine," a senior Congress leader and former Union minister says.

***

Coming after the Chai pe Charcha blitzkrieg – which helped created the impression of Modi being a citizen politician battle-ready to take on governance odds and to highlight social and political issues – the 3D hologram campaign was yet another major coup. It had been tried out earlier in the 2012 Gujarat assembly elections.

The idea came from cinematographer UK Senthil Kumar after his chance meeting with the Gujarat chief minister before the 2012 polls. The 3D hologram campaign involved shooting Modi's speech using 3D holographic technology to enable millions of people to see and hear him from multiple locations. Typically used by rock stars and celebrities in their performances, this technology had never been tried by politicians in India before. Modi, a technology freak, was instantly impressed by the hologram technology and allowed Senthil Kumar, trained in holographic technology in London, to try it out.

The 3D hologram campaign, or 3D rallies, showed Modi appearing out of the blue, in thin air, and speaking to common people. In the Indian countryside as well as cities, this novel concept set in motion talk about Modi long after the rally ended – elevating him from mere mortal to someone with more extraordinary abilities, especially to the uneducated mind. In the assembly elections of 2012, before Modi began his speech in a typical 3D rally, an invisible moderator introduced the people of the state in Gujarati and English to the idea of public addresses using "3D holographic volumetric projection technology". She argued that through the use of such technology in elections, Gujarat had set a new trend for the world to uphold along the lines of the Gujarat development model. Modi's 3D avatar would then appear on stage in a flashy setting. He would begin his speech following a few minutes of songs that kicked up regional pride. "*Bharat Mata Ki...* *Bharat Mata Ki*," he thundered before launching into his usual rousing delivery. "It was a major plus to our campaign. In areas where we didn't have much organisational strength and where there was a lot of infighting among our workers, this 3D campaign breathed a new life," BJP leader Laxmikant Bajpai told me before the polls. Modi, in fact, had attracted a lot of criticism over the use of holograms in the national poll race. Opposition parties had asked the Election Commission to probe the source of funding for the highly expensive hi-tech 3D extravaganza. Congress leaders charged that Rs 5 crore had been spent for each 3D projection that helped Modi speak to voters in rural hamlets normally by-passed by the election process, giving the BJP an edge that other parties could not afford. They argued that all the 'imaginative' techniques used by BJP were nothing more than the ostentatious display of corporate wealth. BJP, of course, denied all accusations.

In fact, political commentator and columnist Swapan Dasgupta had reasoned in an interview that Modi's obsession with technology was necessitated by his long years of lack of popularity in traditional media. Modi had been an early adopter of social media and other alternative channels to communicate with the public because of newspaper and television criticism over his handling of the 2002 Gujarat riots in which more than 1,000 people were killed. "This is another way to reach out to people on his own terms," he was quoted as saying in *The Telegraph*, UK. The most famous hologram show – besides Modi's – has been a posthumous performance by American rapper Tupac Shakur who died in 1996 after he was shot several times in a drive-by shooting in Las Vegas.

Modi's 3D rallies were held in 1,300 locations across India, the first being held on 11 April 2014 and the last on 9 May. Holograms were ten feet tall and their deployment required use of shipping containers, trucks, buses and close to 4,000 workers. Four workers died in road accidents as the Modi election machinery unfurled logistical and technological operations unprecedented in Indian politics.

The CAG team boasts that they created a world record of sorts by holding such events in 150 locations simultaneously on a single day. These rallies created frenzy in many parts of the country where people thronged to take in Modi appearing as if in an epiphany. "It was technology, but people thought there was more to it than technology. If it was just technology then why weren't Rahul or Sonia or Mulayam Singh Yadav appearing out of the blue? people asked. The 3D rallies were therefore a major fillip to our campaign," argues Bajpai. It was, in fact, yet another gigantic vessel of the campaign fleet that, besides capturing people's imagination of Modi being a dogged pursuer, contributed to shaping the idea of a technologically ingenious man who could be the next prime minister of India.

"I think, among the major campaigns, the one that had the greatest impact was the 3D campaign. That was the biggest thing we were involved in," says a CAG member, adding, "Most of our volunteers and members were involved in it. Apart from regular campaign support – which we were providing in terms of surveys, doing the analytics, mobilising volunteers for the different events, helping MPs and candidates at the local level, organising the events, planning, monitoring, giving training to the booth managers and all – apart from all these things, this was one of the biggest campaigns that we ever ran. It was entirely run by the CAG network." The team had a person stationed in each constituency wherever a rally was scheduled to happen.

It was a massive exercise indeed, one India has never seen before. And managing the logistics was a painstaking effort. Organising a 3D rally involved multiple vendors, right from the team that set up the stage to the one that handled satellite connection. Equipment needed to be carried around in trucks that would also house the hologram projector. Coordinating with the projector operator across destinations was an uphill task. He needed assistance from a UPS operator and often a logistics guy to ensure smooth functioning of all equipment. Towards the end of the campaign – which also involved getting permissions, mobilising party cadres and managing everything centrally – there were 150 trucks on the road. Compared with the Gujarat elections, the campaign team tripled the number of

3D rallies it organised on a day from an average of fifty to 150 in the national elections.

"We had made a checklist of every 3D location – and three days in advance, we had to assess the viability, feasibility and suitability of holding a 3D rally at a particular place, similar to the Chai pe Charcha campaign. But the problem here was far more complex because the technology itself was very cumbersome, besides the frequency of running the campaign every alternate day for almost a month," another CAG executive told me.

Poll managers had to factor in all likely hindrances from lack of road connectivity to bad weather. For instance, on 14 April 2014, a storm kicked up in Uttar Pradesh, just three hours before the programme was to start. "As soon as we saw it in Lucknow, we called our people and said, 'Boss, get everything down, let the storm pass'. But we also had our plan B ready. So we called up a few people and we had these cranes come in. These actually picked up the trucks on which the projector was fixed, and at the very last moment, we had eleven locations live out of the twelve that were otherwise completely devastated in the storm." The point he makes is that the team had to stretch themselves a lot more than they had bargained for. "We had to be on our guard all the time," explains a CAG member, adding that attendance at these rallies in Uttar Pradesh could go up to 15,000-20,000 people per event.

The most valuable part of this campaign was that it got covered extensively in the media. The sheer novelty factor drew in TV channels and print journalists who often reported back breathlessly on the goings-on at the events, further gripping the imaginations of lakhs of television viewers and newspaper readers across the country. Television footage of 3D rallies relayed Modi speaking on a variety of subjects, often unsheathing his biting criticism of Congress leaders, especially Rahul Gandhi whom he invariably referred to as the "prince".

***

While most BJP campaign schemes were run across the Hindi belt and beyond, especially the 3D rallies and Chai pe Charcha, it was decided that Uttar Pradesh, which accounts for eighty of the 543

Lok Sabha seats, would be covered through a special project that would take the PM candidate's message to villages not covered much via TV and the Internet. This initiative, started around the time of Holi 2014, continued alongside other big-ticket campaigns until the end of the poll campaign, silently reaping gains for the Hindu nationalist party in the UP where 40-50 percent of its one lakh villages have been described as 'media dark'. This exercise called for making video clips that carried the message of Modi to the people of Uttar Pradesh. CDs were prepared by CAG in consultation with the BJP leadership. The video clips were of ten to fifteen minutes duration.

The *'Modi Aane Wala Hain* (Modi is coming)' (MAWH) campaign envisaged covering nearly 40,000 backward media-dark villages of Uttar Pradesh through small vans – Tata Ace was used for the purpose – that would carry videos of Modi's speeches, and posters and tutorials on how to vote for Modi. Most of these villages were connected through narrow dirt roads. Some 400 video vans were pressed into service and each would ferry one person who operated the video and publicity material and one CAG volunteer. Drivers were selected assessing their familiarity with the region and all these vans were GPS-tagged so that anyone in the war room in Gandhinagar, Gujarat, or a control room of sorts in Lucknow, UP, could identify where each vehicle was at any point of time.

Volunteers reported a strange problem: Most people they surveyed in their villages and hometowns in UP supported Modi. However, a mischievous campaign, as mentioned earlier, launched by rival parties such as SP and BSP misinformed the illiterate villagers of backward areas that if they wanted to vote for Modi, they needed to press the cycle or the elephant symbol on the electronic voting machine. While the elephant is BSP's symbol, the cycle is that of SP. "The villagers were blatantly misguided. Someone would say to an old woman, *'Dadi*, whom do you want to vote for?' and she would say, 'Modi', and they would say, 'Okay, press the bicycle symbol'. So our job was connecting Modi's name to the lotus symbol," says a CAG member.

Thus, MAWH's key priorities included instructing people *how*

to vote for Modi. The central team created slogans for the purpose.
Two of them were:

Do baatein mat jaana bhool
Narendra Modi, kamal ka phool

(Two things you must remember / Narendra Modi, lotus flower)
and

Narendra Modi ko pradhan mantri banana hai
Toh kamal par button dabana hai

(If you want to make Narendra Modi the prime minister /
remember to press the lotus flower)

Eventually, the Modi team rolled out 400 video vans in two
phases and ended up exceeding its target by covering nearly 95,000
of UP's villages. Though not as colourful as Chai pe Charcha and 3D
rallies, it was a mammoth project, a BJP leader says. "From managing
entry permits from district magistrates to tackling problems arising
out of the driver of a van being beaten up by a rival party member or
the van being burnt by thugs, MAWH was a huge effort and we often
had 100-150 complaints coming our way every week. We also had a
helpline number," says a Modi campaign team member. "We had set
up a couple of televisions there in the Lucknow central office of
the BJP, where Amit Shah and Sunil Bansal used to monitor villages
covered by MAWH campaigners," he adds. According to estimates,
these vehicles reached out to six-seven crore people covering more
than six lakh kilometres throughout this campaign.

The slogan, *Modi Aane Wala Hai*, really rocked, says Laxmikant
Bajpai, president of BJP's Uttar Pradesh unit. "It created much buzz
among the people of UP and also energised the cadre," says another
BJP leader from the state. Villagers would often talk to acquaintances
in neighbouring hamlets, talking as if Modi himself had planned a
visit to them – "Yesterday, Modi had come," or "Tomorrow, Modi is
coming". Words that were music to campaign managers' ears.

The BJP's PM aspirant soon acquired a halo and so did Brand
Modi.

***

The public shenanigans on display during Election 2014 were the
result of not just front-office efforts, but also meticulous backbone

building with data mining. The RSS and BJP outdid even themselves in this regard.

Many data-management firms got busy in number-crunching and data collection that could be put to use in the 2014 general election, a majority of these being pro-BJP. Rajesh Jain of Mumbai-based Netcore Solutions – who had hogged headlines when he sold Internet portal IndiaWorld to Satyam Computer Services in a multi-crore transaction in the mid-1990s – returned to the media limelight when his company collected fourteen million phone numbers in the anti-corruption movement led by Anna Hazare in 2011.

Supriya Sharma wrote in Scroll.in: "Lakhs of people turned up to support (the Anna Hazare-led) India Against Corruption (IAC). But an even greater number who could not come to the (Ramlila) Maidan took an easier route to expressing their support: they gave a missed call on 022-61550789. IAC had advertised the number and had asked people to leave a missed call to register their support. The idea worked. In less than three months, more than 7.6 million people called. Within six months, twenty-five million missed calls had been logged in."

That database of numbers, which was in IAC's custody, comprising people across all walks of life, including taxi drivers and janitors and washerwomen, was collected using a software developed by Netcore which could also track down data on the caller's geographical location and other details.

By 2013, the managing director and founder of the award-winning company, Jain, had joined the Modi bandwagon as one of the many experts who would lead the online campaign for Modi. In response to journalists on whether the IAC database would be made available to the BJP team, Jain, then forty-six, was emphatic that it would not.

Jain, an Internet entrepreneur and an alumnus of IIT Bombay and Columbia University, has always been a champion of political entrepreneurship, suggesting that ordinary people should get a say in governance and in combating corruption. An ardent fan of Modi, he argued that Modi's Gujarat was a shining example of a state that has put integrity and development above everything else.

"If only we could get Modi to run the country for five years... is the common refrain," he wrote on his blog. Jain, according to a BJP functionary, had met American presidential election experts to consult them on how strategies used in the US could be adapted to ensure a presidential-type election win for Modi in India. His efforts were not only meant to help Modi in the 2014 election but to streamline systems for elections years down the line. "He did many things to test the waters, to see how strategies used elsewhere could be replicated here," a person close to him told me.

After having praised Modi lavishly, Jain began to help the PM candidate in his campaign through Internet and phone-based campaigns. His efforts ran parallel to those of BG Mahesh, founder of Greynisum Information Technologies, who would later play a pivotal role in PM Modi's digital media policy team. According to a BJP leader, Jain and his team also went on to create a "digital database" of eighty-one crore voters of the country that otherwise lies scattered around in physical format and in numerous regional languages. The task was monumental, though some leaders wondered what use would a long list of names of all the country's voters have for any political party in the short term – after all, the electoral roll is available online.

Dr Vijay Chauthaiwale, however, shares that Jain's genius lay in linking the usual information available on the electoral roll with the voters' mobile numbers. These had been collected from lakhs of citizens through the NaMo number campaign. The campaign was designed to generate support amongst cellular phone users for Modi. Voters had to send a message to 7820078200 with the voter ID number of the user and the number of the Modi supporter motivating him or her to send the message as a suffix.

In return, the phone user would get a message about the details of his polling booth and encouragement to take his friends and family along to vote. The purpose was two-fold: One was getting the mobile number of a voter and linking it with his or her voter ID number. The other was getting a grip on the total number of voters each BJP party worker had influenced. The tally of each worker – called the NaMo number – was put up on a website. Designed like a multi-level marketing scheme, the system gave points for those who relayed the right message down the line. "If not at the booth level, Jain had certainly analysed voter numbers down to the block level," says Chauthaiwale.

Jain, however, came under scathing criticism from the rabidly anti-Modi website, TruthOfGujarat.com. The website's writers Mukesh Sinha and Pratik Sinha wrote that pro-Modi websites, India272.com, GujaratRiots.com, NitiCentral.com, BJPOne.com, et cetera, were being run by Jain's team, officially appointed by Modi to run his IT campaign. "Their common roots can be seen from the fact that each one of these websites reside on the same server with the IP Address 206.183.107.25. Rajesh Jain's blog Emergic.Org is also one of these several sites sitting on this server. India272.com which is regularly endorsed by Narendra Modi on Twitter also sits on this same server," they wrote on 6 October 2013. They further maligned Jain: "Netcore (had) acquired OneIndia.in website, which became a primary vehicle for Modi's NRI propaganda. Modi also made him the director of Gujarat Informatics Limited around 2011 and it was ever since then that Rajesh Jain has been spawning website after website for promoting the political fortunes of Modi." Jain and his team denied allegations of any wrongdoing.

Jain refused to be interviewed for this book, saying that he didn't want to talk about the 2014 election. While India272.com now directs a surfer to mygov.in, a government website which invites comments and suggestions on various official projects from people, Jain stays low-profile. In the run-up to the polls, Kishor-led CAG gained an edge over Jain's team and, of course, so did the BJP's IT cell headed by Arvind Gupta, thanks to its out-of-the-box ideas and skilful execution of programmes such as Chai pe Charcha and 3D rallies besides other crucial poll campaigns. In the game of one-upmanship among these expert campaigners owing allegiance to Modi, Kishor gained a clear lead towards the end, outshining all campaigns by rivals. "It is Kishor's team that contributed the most to the 2014 poll strategy, especially with their innovative forms of campaigning that took Modi closer to people… I would say that had it not been for Kishor and to some extent people like Jain, Congress would have still been able to put up a good fight," a BJP leader who worked very closely with national leaders in Delhi told me.

***

A large part of BJP's hype-creating machinery was dependent on the massive amounts of data they managed to collect, sort and digitise. Though Jain's team had compiled a list of eighty-one lakh voters and connected many mobile phone numbers with voter IDs, it was the CAG team that ruled the data-collecting game, down to nearly six lakh booths across the country.

CAG's data-analytics team helped BJP in two major ways. One, they managed to collect booth-wise performance of political parties over the past eight elections – including the state and national polls. Two, they were able to segregate each and every constituency based on its prospects for the BJP – which was of great use for the RSS, a leader of the organisation told me, emphasising that it made RSS and the BJP sit up about their performance in several constituencies. "We had not done that badly after all. We do have a chance this time around, especially in many seats of Uttar Pradesh," he said at the time of the elections. Similar data collection was attempted by others, too, but it was the one CAG compiled that the RSS found useful.

The CAG analytics team digitised the election results with a clear-cut plan, says a member. "It was done to remove biases of previous elections. Every seat in India was slotted into one of four categories based on their probabilities to win, or their current status. The categories were: safe (BJP seat assured), favourable (tending towards the BJP, yet it could swing the other way too), battleground (where it is a neck-and-neck fight), and difficult (traditional rival seat)," explains a CAG member. Interestingly, Varanasi fell in the 'favourable' zone, and not 'safe' because calculations were based on retrospective data. "After all, this election was very different from the usual: it was a wave," he adds.

This kind of data-crunching also meant that the BJP and the RSS got invaluable data at the village level. "The booth-wise picture helped us plan accordingly – where did we need to recruit more people for door-to-door canvassing? Where did we need to assign special squads to track the work of the rivals and counter them? Everything suddenly became very scientific. Earlier, we based our planning on mental calculations. This time, we had data on our fingertips, literally, on a sheet of paper," says a senior RSS leader from Lucknow.

The logic behind the CAG analytics can be explained this way: suppose you have 1,000 resources, what is the best way to distribute them among the districts? If it's a safe seat, there's no point in Modi visiting twice or thrice for canvassing votes. This information was put to best use during the Bharat Vijay rallies – on-ground grand events where Modi tore into the Congress – where locations were mostly chosen through CAG's categorisation. "It helped tremendously in suggesting which spots to hit and which ones to miss," says a Modi team member. Though it was BJP and not CAG that took the final call on deciding rally venues, CAG's data helped in choosing seats that needed the attention of topnotch campaigners.

Beginning 26 March 2014, Modi addressed 196 Bharat Vijay rallies across 295 Lok Sabha constituencies during the elections – all of them identified by CAG as crucial – and about 450 in the run-up to the state elections that preceded the Lok Sabha elections. Team Modi also paid attention to multiple nearby locations in the zone of 'battleground' seats to usher in a spillover effect while scheduling Modi's visits. A CAG member told me that they followed a very "complex yet effective model" in choosing rally spots: "When we went to BJP with this plan and told them to follow this schedule, they could not move even a single location from here to there. If you change even one, it ruins the plan for the next one, and it goes on like a domino effect. Modi followed it almost exactly, barring last-minute diversions and requests from high-profile candidates." One out-of- turn rally Modi addressed was in Amethi, a difficult seat where he needn't have gone, says a BJP leader. "Of course, some subjective calls are always taken," he adds.

There were other constraints as well. One was that Modi had to return to Gandhinagar every night. Another was that he had to be in two regions on a single day to sustain buzz around the country. The idea was that the local media should have something to write every day. But even the various stretches of Modi's travel time were put to good use – sitting in his helicopter or flight or car from one venue to another, he would catch up on notes prepared for him by his team.

These notes were instant compilations of the news of the day besides local factors – such as key communities to appeal to and highly relevant local issues. CAG would give a chart-sheet with inputs to Modi's office for every rally. "We would point out the main five news points about the particular constituency he was heading to. Who is the leader? What is the political scenario there? What are the key communities that you need to appeal to?" says a member. This list was also sent to the parliamentary constituency (PC) coordinator before each rally.

The Delhi war room, led by the likes of Manoj Ladwa and Vijay Chauthaiwale, also alerted Modi's secretary who accompanied him on tour, Om Prakash, if there was a statement from a Congress leader that had to be countered in the next rally. "This in-between-rallies briefing helped sustain the momentum of tit-for-tat exchanges in which Modi was always leaps ahead of his rivals," a BJP leader based in Gandhinagar says. During the height of the election, a team of two was exclusively assigned to monitoring Sonia Gandhi's and Rahul Gandhi's speeches – jumping in on any faux pas or comment criticising the BJP. Within ten minutes after their speech ended, Modi's team would come up with a bullet-point summary of eight to ten points – including pro-UPA claims and anti-BJP/NDA remarks – and shoot it off to Modi.

Modi was also briefed about what *not* to speak at rallies. "Modi himself suggested that we include a 'don't say' category in our briefings for him," says the CAG member, laughing meaningfully.

The video coverage of Modi's rallies was also put to good use. The digital feeds were immediately edited by CAG and selective 'good snippets' were passed on to a coordinator to upload on WhatsApp – volunteers further distributed these amongst their individual networks. A summary of the rally would be compiled and sent out as well. The CAG team also sent bulk messages to each person who had attended the rally with a note of thanks. The online poll campaigners also connected with trolls and other BJP sympathisers.

They urged them to disseminate the content on their web pages. With some of them enjoying close to half a million views, this was a valuable resource CAG could not afford to miss.

***

Another CAG activity proved exceedingly useful. These were pre-poll interviews. Around fifty to sixty people were extensively interviewed in each of the 200 to 250 Lok Sabha seats identified by CAG, starting from April 2014. The idea was to know the thoughts and opinions of the key influencers in each PC, and so the persons interviewed were selected across professions, castes and classes.

Interestingly, such interviews helped CAG members to come up with stunning forecasts. For instance, in Bhagalpur, Bihar, after conducting several in-depth interviews and surveys, CAG volunteers came up with certain data, collated by their central team, which predicted that BJP leader Shahnawaz Hussain was going to lose. This feedback was given to the state leadership of Patna and to Hussain himself. But the state leadership ignored warnings and did not stretch itself to try to cover lost ground; it was very confident of winning from Bhagalpur. CAG sent a second warning report and it was once again ignored.

Eventually, Hussain lost.

Similarly, CAG surveys from the North-Central Mumbai seat predicated that BJP's Poonam Mahajan would win. But local leaders insisted that it was a difficult task and that this seat was taken: after all, Priya Dutt of the Congress had been doing very well in the area for years. "No, we cannot win it!" a Maharashtra BJP leader told CAG, emphatically, arguing that further campaigning would be useless.

But Mahajan won by a margin of 1.86 lakh votes, beating Dutt who had represented that particular PC for two terms – a win that left BJP speechless in euphoria.

Another big task CAG undertook was a concept called 'social listening' in each of the forty Lok Sabha constituencies in Bihar. They sent trained people to track each caste's political affinity in each PC. These volunteers would visit different tea stalls, talk to local people and make a structured report. "That data was very crucial and useful in Bihar because elections are caste-based in the state much more than anywhere else," says a BJP leader. "I think the contribution of this feedback to poll wins in Bihar was significant," BJP's Dharmendra Pradhan, now Union minister, had told me just after the results came out. He was the central leader in charge of the state where the BJP alliance won thirty-one of the forty seats.

Poll triumph in Bihar, like in Uttar Pradesh, was hugely significant in that it saw several senior members of rival parties biting the dust. Rashtriya Janata Dal (RJD) chief Lalu Prasad's wife Rabri Devi lost to Rajiv Pratap Rudy of the BJP in the high-profile Saran seat. In Patliputra, Prasad's daughter Misa Bharti suffered defeat at the hands of Ramkripal Yadav of the BJP.

Take into account the extent of discipline and implementation of poll programmes, and the boys at CAG do walk away with a lot of credit in BJP's election win of 2014. But their leader Kishor – who loves arguments and despises lackadaisical work attitudes – isn't the quintessential political animal. With a squat gym physique, tough stance and studiedly casual attire – he was wearing a blue chest-hugging T-shirt, navy jeans and blue Nike shoes when I met him – he says he has only one role model in politics, Mahatma Gandhi, whose greatness he discovered only after years of being taught to dislike him. It was when he began working for the UN in Europe and Africa that he realised the incomparable greatness of the father of the nation. Now he is in awe of the Mahatma, and nobody else matters. Kishor refuses to discuss his friendship with Modi and declines to talk about what he plans to do for him next.

His boys at CAG, in the meantime, have drawn up a list of fifteen areas where they could possibly invest their time and effort now that the elections are over. With thousands of volunteers itching to work with them again, they have key categories like healthcare, skill development and education on their agenda. "Our group's actual purpose – Citizens for Accountable Governance – is to get citizens involved in nation-building activity. We plan to leverage the resources that we've already developed so far," they say, enthusiastically. "Everyone wants to do this at some point or the other. We are trying to be there for them." The boys have yet to develop the air of cynicism their leader sports. For now, their idealism is contagious.

Notes

1. Pub. HarperCollins Publishers India, 2013, New Delhi.

2. Telecast on 27 January 2014 on Times Now, the interview of Rahul Gandhi by Arnab Goswami, editor-in-chief of Times Now, turned out to be a public-relations disaster for the Nehru-Gandhi scion. He avoided answering Goswami's questions on the Congress's role in the 1984 anti-Sikh riots, and appeared ignorant about the facts of the 2002 Gujarat riots even while trying to compare the two. Though he tried to draw attention to a few key issues such as the empowerment of women and uplift of the poor, his demeanour came across as immature, underconfident and clueless of important political events. The *New York Times* later said, "Mr Gandhi fumbled, stared with a blank expression and a tilted head and looked wounded at times."

5 | NAMO
"Ambition is not a dirty word. Piss on compromise. Go for the throat."

– Steven Erikson, Gardens of the Moon

It was an unremarkable morning when a fellow journalist and I arrived at Ahmedabad's supremely crowded railway station by an overnight train from Mumbai. We were to leave for Udaipur, the tourist hub in neighbouring Rajasthan, along with other bachelor friends the same evening for a few days of basking in the winter sun, beer in hand, enjoying a well-earned holiday. The date was 27 February 2002.

Instead, as fate would have it, we could not leave the city. We returned to Mumbai on a despondent night journey more than a week later, shaken and, I have to admit, emotionally bruised.

Around the same time that we arrived in Ahmedabad with nothing but having a good time on our minds, another train carrying, among others, Hindu pilgrims from Ayodhya – the birthplace of Lord Ram where a mosque built in the sixteenth century by destroying a temple was demolished by Right-wing Hindu fanatics in 1992 – arrived at a station two and half hours away. The Sabarmati Express was running late by five hours when it reached the Godhra railway station at 7:43 a.m. A mob, comprising mostly Muslims, attacked the pilgrims and set fire to coach S-6, killing fifty-nine people, including twenty-five women and fifteen children. When the train had come to a halt at the railway station in Godhra, which is 40 percent Muslim and prone to religious violence, the pilgrims had reportedly chanted religious slogans that first led to a scuffle and then arson, some reports suggested.

This was before the widespread use of mobile Internet, Twitter and news apps, and we were clueless about the events happening nearby as we went about in search of a bootlegger to stock up on the requisite alcohol for our getaway – Gujarat is a 'dry' state, where Prohibition has been in place for decades; there are of course a few legal 'permit rooms' where you can buy drinks if you submit proof of residence outside the state. Ordinary travellers like us had neither the patience nor wherewithal to do so, and had no choice but to resort to the many bootleggers who, naturally, ran a thriving business in the state.

We found out about the Godhra train incident only on our return to our friend's home where, sensing trouble, we decided to stay the night. The next day, blaming Muslims for killing the pilgrims, Hindu mobs, allegedly with the connivance of the government, went on a rampage of destruction, raping, killing and looting Muslim neighbourhoods in a spasm of violence that would last two months. Muslims also hit back in some pockets. About 800 Muslims and 250 Hindus were killed in the bloodiest riots in India in the twenty-first century, according to official figures. Some 20,000 Muslim homes and businesses and 360 places of worship were destroyed, and roughly 1.5 lakh people were displaced.

Amidst all the chaos, one memory stands out. A ten-year-old boy in the upper-class Hindu-dominated neighbourhood where we were staying was taken on a tour of the city by his father, mainly to parts where Muslims were being hunted down by mobs. The idea of this "riots tourism" was to make a man out of this boy, and, as his mother explained to us, to prepare him to withstand any kind of "frightening sights". There was something eerily Ku Klux Klannish about that behaviour, I thought. The extent and depth of polarisation along religious lines in Gujarat, the western Indian state that is home to prosperous merchants and numerous entrepreneurs, worried me. It is a state that has seen a lot of migration of Hindus

and Muslims overseas where they tend to live in harmony. What was
wrong with this place? Would the riots spread to Mumbai and other
parts of India? I wondered.

My friend Prem Udayabhanu had to shave off his flourishing
beard for fear of being wrongly identified as a Muslim – there
was a rumour that the only bearded man safe in Gujarat was then
Chief Minister Modi whose police officers were not seen anywhere
in the initial days after the Godhra incident as the mayhem spread
rapidly. There were violent groups everywhere attacking and looting
Muslims. Instead of policemen, in the first three days of the riots,
we saw motorbike-bound men wearing saffron bandanas, surveying
and guarding Hindu areas when they were not targeting Muslims.
When a relatively posh restaurant we frequented was gutted down,
we realised it was a 'Muslim shop', owned by a couple living in the
US. The two biggest massacres, we knew later, happened in Naroda
Patiya, where more than ninety people were killed, and at the Gulbarg
Society, an upper-class Muslim housing complex in Ahmedabad
where poor Muslims had taken refuge. Former Congress lawmaker
Ehsan Jafri, who, it is believed, had made several attempts to contact
the police, was among the sixty-nine people who died there. Jafri was
first hacked to death and then burnt.

Modi, who had assumed the office of chief minister just five
months earlier, was accused of condoning the violence. It triggered,
rightfully or otherwise, a die-hard obsession among the media,
intellectuals and rival politicians at home and in the West with the
cult of villainy surrounding him. It took him a long time to blunt
that image. Paradoxically, it gave him the irresistible appeal of the
Hindu alpha male, helping him easily rustle his way to become the
undisputed leader of the Hindu nationalist BJP, who for a section of
Hindu majority symbolised the exceptional qualities of bravery and
chivalry the likes of Maharana Pratap and Shivaji – who had resisted
the Islamist invasion of India – were known for. He would benefit
from a political posturing that had earlier benefited the BJP during
the Ayodhya movement, something that author Christophe Jaffrelot
had called "the reactivation of a Hindu sentiment of vulnerability".
Hindus in India still suffer from an inferiority complex of having

been '*ghulam* (slave)' to invaders, meaning Muslim rulers and the British. Exploiting that wounded pride has been the cornerstone of the BJP's politics. American philosopher Martha C. Nussbaum, who has studied Modi's campaigns in a book called *The Clash Within*,[1] told me in an interview that Modi has always appealed to fear, and often plays on the apprehensions of the Muslim minority. "There is also an appeal to shame, since the sense was conveyed, at least in pamphlets circulated prior to the 2002 riots [whether with Modi's direct participation or not] that Hindu men have been weak and passive, and are therefore in a shamefully dominated position. They need to learn to stand up for themselves, aggressively if necessary," she told me.

The negative reactions that the 2002 riots evoked, rendering Modi a political pariah of sorts, put him in a phase of trial by fire – and by the time he emerged unscathed, the chorus for his elevation as the prime ministerial candidate grew so great that the RSS couldn't afford not to take note of the groundswell of support building up within and without.

How did Modi tackle near insurmountable odds? There are those in his party who believe that it was in his stars to be what he is today. But then it is unfair to overlook Modi's vaulting ambitions and his all-out efforts to chase his goals.

***

More than 100 kilometres away from Ahmedabad stands Vadnagar, where you don't see any of the prosperity and rich cultural links Chinese traveller Hiuen Tsang had talked about when he visited this town, then called Anandapura, in 641 AD. Many centuries later in 1950, when Modi was born as the third of six children to Damodardas Mulchand Modi and his wife Heeraben, it was an impoverished, decrepit Gujarati town populated by working-class families. Modi's family, from a backward Ghanchi caste, lived in a house along the narrow alleys here. Their livelihood came from crushing oil seeds to make oil and selling it in the local markets. They had to cut corners to make both ends meet. To make extra money, his father also ran a teashop at the Vadnagar railway station and as a schoolboy, Narendra would skip classes to assist his father sell tea to commuters.

In the shanties that serve tea along Vadnagar's narrow roads, people today appear perpetually wonderstruck. They have been fed various heroic tales of the BJP heavyweight dating back to his childhood ever since he became Gujarat's chief minister some thirteen years ago. Some of these tales have become part of Modi mythology, such as the story of the teenaged Narendra's escape from the jaws of a crocodile in the nearby Sharmishtha Lake, which is fed by water from the river Kapila known to nourish the earliest settlement in this region. The story of Modi's escape from a crocodile echoes the childhood experience of Jagatguru Adi Shankaracharya, the great Hindu seer who lived and died in Varanasi.

Modi attended Bhagavatacharya Narayanacharya High School where he was an average student. He visited this place recently, a guard at the entrance told me. Modi's Sanskrit teacher Prahlad Patel had seen nothing extraordinary about Modi, except that he was active in debates and in theatre. After school hours, he regularly attended the *shakha* meetings of the RSS from the age of eight. Some friends of his remember Modi as an active kid, who loved beating friends in impromptu swimming contests at the Sharmishtha Lake. He was also passionate about flying kites; watching the rise of a little strip of paper through the expansive skies, cutting down others that came in its path, perhaps echoed his own aspirations. Though Modi would leave his hometown at a young age and detach himself from close association with members of his family, he remained enamoured of the long history of the place. Hiuen Tsang had written about the Buddhist monasteries here, and recent excavations in Vadnagar have proved its deep Buddhist connections. During the recent visit of Chinese President Xi Jinping, Modi flaunted Vadnagar's history in a slide show prepared by his government.

When I met HK Mehta, a businessman and the brother of local BJP leader Sunil Mehta, he said he had never seen Modi as a child – when Modi joined the local school, Mehta had already passed out from there. Besides, how could someone know a person from such a background when he was a child, he asks. Which is why he is disinterested in "the ballads" that have surfaced about Modi's extraordinary childhood feats and heroics. He would like to focus

more on the Modi he really knew: Mehta first met him when he gave
a speech "some twenty-five years ago". By then, Modi had left home,
wandered the Himalayas, learnt Swami Vivekananda's quotations
by heart, grown a beard on the advice of a saint, became a full-
time member of the RSS and had his now-famous 56-inch chest. "I
looked at his forehead and I knew he was a born leader," Mehta told
me. He says he derives immense pride in seeing Modi become one
of India's tallest politicians.

Without doubt, Modi the RSS volunteer didn't want to join his
parents in their traditional jobs of either oil-pressing or tea-selling.
Unlike most of his peers – which included his five siblings – in this
sleepy semi-rural outpost, Modi was ambitious and had no qualms
about it. He was different from other children his age: he was
deeply affected by India's wars of 1962 and 1965 and wanted to do
something for his country.

Young Modi was inspired by Swami Vivekananda's teachings
which also stressed spiritual and physical strength – and that could
explain Modi's obsession with physical fitness. Out of a spiritual
quest that came from being fed on such books, he left home when
he was barely eighteen. This was around the time that he was married
in accordance with a tradition of childhood betrothal still common
in his community to Jashoda Chimanlal Modi, the seventeen-year-
old daughter of schoolteacher Chimanlal and his wife Sakri*ben* Modi.
Modi didn't bother to honour his marital commitments and travelled
to the Belur Math in West Bengal and beyond, destined never to live
in Vadnagar again.

Modi always kept his family away from media glare and also
from his offices. He trumpeted this as an achievement of sorts,
saying that he has no family to care for unlike the rival opposition
party, Congress, which is run largely by the Nehru-Gandhi clan
where leadership is based on dynastic privileges. He is known to have
trained himself at detachment, something that sets him apart from
most politicians who often have permanent friends and enemies.

All these behavioural aberrations surprised Modi's kin, who
had expected him to live a happy married life in Vadnagar. When
Modi's mother, now ninety-four, asked him in the early 1970s where

he had been for two years, he said he had been on a self-imposed exile "in the Himalayas". Modi had been associated closely with the Ramakrishna Mission, both in West Bengal and Rajkot, in Gujarat, where an ascetic, Swami Atmasthananda, advised him not to become a Mission monk, insisting that his calling lay elsewhere. According to Modi's biographer Andy Marino, who had great access to the leader while working for his book, *Narendra Modi: A Political Biography*,[2] the BJP leader met Atmasthananda in 2013 at the Belur Math to thank him for that advice.

Though he made a visit to his mother who lives in Gandhinagar with one of his brothers for a photo-op before leaving for Delhi for his swearing-in as prime minister, he didn't bring her to the capital for the colourful ceremony. A few days after becoming prime minister, he visited his mother again on his sixty-fourth birthday, an army of photographers and TV crew filming their every move. While his frail mother Hiraba was visibly delighted in his company, unable to take her eyes off his face, Modi's own demeanour was criticised as arrogant and "put-on".

Modi's lack of affinity towards the family is well-known. One of his brothers, Prahlad, who runs a small tyre shop in Ahmedabad, had told BBC that looking after his family is not Modi's priority. He said with a sense of regret, "I wish he would help the next generation of our family. But I am sure he won't. He won't even offer tea to someone without a reason – especially his family." Modi's marriage to Jashoda*ben* was also a neglected beast. After their wedding, the teenaged Jashoda had moved back to her father's home and completed her schooling; she then went on to become a primary schoolteacher, finally retiring from the Rajosana Primary School at the age of fifty-eight. Haima Deshpande of *OPEN* magazine had interviewed her in her home in Rajosana village in 2009. Deshpande found that she lived in a one-room tenement in the Panchalvas area in the village, and paid a rent of Rs 150 every month. The 100 sq ft room she lived in had a tin roof and no toilet, not even a bathroom. The tap was located outside the house. After her retirement, she moved in with her brothers and their families in Brahmanvada village. In an interview to the *Indian Express* published on 1 February 2014,

Jashoda*ben* explained that she bore no grudge against her husband for keeping her a secret, saying it was part of his "destiny". On the other hand, his family has been highly supportive of him. Modi, who had to declare himself as a married man when the nomination papers for the Vadodara Lok Sabha constituency were filed in the 2014 elections, immediately received flak for abandoning a woman after marrying her and for not taking care of her. His brother Soma*bhai* Damodardas Modi came to his defence, saying Modi was married to Jashoda*ben* more than forty-five years ago when he was a minor and the family was poor and uneducated. Soma*bhai* justified Modi's decision to snap all ties with his wife, arguing that he had given up family for the country's service. Soma*bhai* also appealed to voters to not judge Modi on the basis of his past. Within months of Modi becoming PM, Jashoda*ben* made her first piece of news when she filed an RTI (Right to Information) demanding a copy of the order that had assigned an armed team of security guards to follow her in air-conditioned vehicles even as she continued using public transport. She also demanded to know what other facilities she was entitled to as the PM's wife. For Modi, Jashoda*ben* is a touchy subject.

However, after initial frustration and hiccups, Modi remained immune to personal onslaught. This emotional aloofness has been the basis of his "extreme defiance". "He owes his rise from a pariah to prime minister – from the quiet backwaters of Vadnagar to Delhi's highly fortified 7 Race Course Road residence – to his own towering ambitions and to the RSS which groomed him into a seasoned organiser," said a BJP leader who has watched him closely for several decades.

***

Through the 1970s and 1980s, Modi worked with the RSS in Gujarat, as well as outside. Having become an active member of the RSS after the Indo-Pakistan War of 1971, he was in charge of recruiting cadres from among the colleges and schools of Gujarat. When then Prime Minister Indira Gandhi imposed a state of Emergency[3] in the country in 1975, suspending elections and curbing civil liberties, he became an active participant of the resistance movement in the state. That was a period when Modi went underground and travelled incognito, disguising himself as a Sikh, a saint, and so on. He was instrumental in distributing leaflets and publicity material exposing the government's atrocities during the Emergency, a period which lasted until 1977. Like most RSS workers, he was active in the "total revolution" movement led by Jayaprakash Narayan. Modi would later write about his Emergency days in a book titled *Sangharsh ma Gujarat* (Gujarat's Struggle). While he was active in the RSS, he also went on to pursue studies at Delhi University and Gujarat University. After the Emergency, Modi rose rapidly in the RSS. His uncanny ability to connect with people won him many friends, including BJP heavyweight LK Advani who was later instrumental in co-opting him to the BJP.

In 1987, he joined the BJP under instructions from Advani and the late RSS leader Kushabhau Thakre. By then, Modi had succeeding in denting the Congress's dominance in several local and municipal bodies in Gujarat. He travelled the length and breadth of the state many times on foot, familiarising himself with its fields, hills and valleys, and befriending party cadres. In January 1992, Modi rose to prominence outside of Gujarat as an intrepid party leader by accompanying Murli Manohar Joshi in his Ekta Yatra.[4]

Many Delhi-based political observers remember coming across Modi's name from a picture that was taken in the New Year of 1992 in Srinagar when Joshi hoisted the national flag in a finale to the 47-day march from Kanyakumari that Kashmiri militants had threatened to disrupt. Prime Minister PV Narasimha Rao's army helped Joshi and his team hoist the flag amid tight security arrangements. The ceremony was over within twelve minutes and the 58-year-old Joshi looked nervous and overwrought. The man who stood next to Joshi, unswerving, defiant and undeterred by the winter chill of Srinagar helping the BJP veteran hoist the flag, was the 42-year-old Modi.

By the time Modi returned to Gujarat, amid talk that he had refused to wear the mandatory body armour while he was in Srinagar for the Ekta Yatra, there was a surge of envy and dislike for Modi's autocratic tendencies and self-promotion among the likes of Shankersinh Vaghela, then the powerful president of the state unit of the BJP. Vaghela and Modi had known each other even before the Emergency. Modi had once sneaked into a jail in Bhavnagar where Vaghela was lodged during the period. But by the 1990s, Vaghela was a staunch rival, who twice ensured that Modi could not step foot in Gujarat for long stretches of time. Notably, it was Advani who would play a very crucial role at this time in Modi's ascent in the organisation despite stiff opposition from the likes of Vaghela.

Modi would later describe those years when he was forced by BJP rivals to work outside Gujarat, first as BJP secretary and later as its general secretary, as the most productive years in his life. Such adversities are opportunities too, he would tell his confidant Amit Shah when the Supreme Court imposed a restriction on the latter's entry to the state.

For Modi, such intervals away from the thick of action in Gujarat meant honing his organisational skills elsewhere. In 1992, facing snubs from the Vaghela camp, he didn't go into a total sulk. He told author Marino that one of the big things he did in this period was to build a school named Sanskardham in Allahabad as homage to his earliest mentor in the RSS, 'Vakil Sahib' Lakshmanrao Inamdar, with whom he had stayed in Ahmedabad's Hedgewar Bhavan. Back then, Modi used to make tea and cook for RSS campaigners, besides mopping the nine rooms in the Bhavan and washing his and Vakil Sahib's clothes.

Once back in Gujarat, Modi grew into an astute politician and a resolute organiser, campaigning extensively in Gujarat in the 1995 assembly polls that elected BJP to power in the western state. But he was soon caught on the wrong side of the power struggle between Vaghela and Keshubhai Patel, the then chief minister and Modi's close ally. Vaghela plotted the exit of Patel along with Sanjay Joshi, who also floated rumours that strained Modi's ties with Patel. Patel was away in the US when Vaghela flew forty-seven MLAs to a luxury hotel in the Madhya Pradesh town of Khajuraho and staked his claim to the chief minister's post with their backing. After Vaghela's revolt, it emerged that Patel didn't enjoy the support of the majority in the BJP legislature party in the Gujarat assembly. A crisis erupted and as soon as Patel returned from the US, the central leadership had to step in to firefight.

Senior BJP leader AB Vajpayee suggested a resolution: Vaghela could not replace Patel. Instead, they would have a compromise chief minister: Suresh Mehta.

But Vaghela and Patel wanted something more: they demanded that the BJP expel Modi from Gujarat because he was the one fanning discontent.

Of course, though Modi left, the warring factions were at it again after a lull and Vaghela's honeymoon in the BJP didn't last long. Fidgety about not being made chief minister, he quit the BJP, floated his own party, Rashtriya Janta Party, secured enough numbers by engineering defections and assumed the post of CM for two years from 1996. In 1998, in a reversal of fortunes that is typical of democratic politics, BJP once again won in Gujarat by a clear margin, marking the return of Keshubhai Patel as CM. Sanjay Joshi, an opportunist to the core who had by then won back Patel's trust, earned plaudits for being a key architect of that victory in Modi's absence. Vaghela later joined the Congress.

In the meantime, outside of Gujarat, Modi grew in the ranks of the party. By 1998, he was elevated to the crucial post of general secretary. Under Modi's watch, the BJP's tally rose to eleven in 1996 from just two in the 1991 Haryana assembly polls. In the Himachal assembly, where BJP had just eight seats when Modi assumed charge, the tally reached thirty-one seats in 1998. As the party's general secretary, Modi also built a wide network in Madhya Pradesh, Chhattisgarh, Rajasthan, Bihar, Jharkhand and Maharashtra. All the while he also bonded with local party workers, leaders and bureaucrats. Party leaders he had befriended would prove to be extremely helpful later in his race to become the prime ministerial candidate of his party.

Over the next decade he would also ensure that Sanjay Joshi would be forced to resign as member of the BJP national executive.

Modi's hostilities with Joshi had only exacerbated over the years with the former rising rapidly to become the party's poster boy. Never one to plot revenge in the conventional way, Modi bade his time before he could get back at Joshi. According to party insiders, the rivalry between Modi and Joshi even resulted in souring of ties between Modi and former BJP President Nitin Gadkari, who had inducted Joshi in his team in 2011 and named him poll manager for Uttar Pradesh. Ahead of the BJP national executive committee meeting in Mumbai in 2012, Modi had reportedly told Gadkari that he would not attend the meeting unless Joshi, who had become a bee in Modi's bonnet, was sacked from the executive committee. Under pressure, Joshi had agreed to resign and Gadkari publicly hailed the decision as "an act of sacrifice" in the interest of the party.

Again, in the run-up to the 2014 polls, when RSS chief Mohan Bhagwat, whose father Madhukar Rao Bhagwat was Modi's mentor in the RSS, insisted on rehabilitating Sanjay Joshi, Modi rejected it, arguing that the 52-year-old had campaigned against him in the past, to the extent of destabilising the party's state unit along with Vaghela in the late 1990s.

Modi never forgave or forgot his enemies.

***

On 1 October 2001, then Prime Minister Atal Bihari Vajpayee called Modi over to meet him. After exchanging pleasantries, Vajpayee brought up the subject of sending Modi back to Gujarat. According to Modi's biographer Marino, Vajpayee made Modi the suggestion that he could take over from Keshubhai Patel and prepare the state for the next assembly polls. Modi said no at first, but agreed to spend ten days a month in Gujarat working among the people.

When Modi returned to Gujarat in 2001 after six years, the government led by an ailing Patel was hurtling from crisis to crisis, buffeted by corruption charges and nepotism. Modi realised within days that Patel's misrule had left the state BJP in disarray. The Patel administration had incurred the people's wrath over the mishandling of the Bhuj earthquake of 2001 that killed more than 20,000 people. It emerged later that many new buildings that were reduced to rubble in Ahmedabad and elsewhere in the state were shoddily built by unscrupulous builders who enjoyed Patel's patronage. The political aftershocks were too intense to ignore. Preparing the party for the elections in December 2002 was not going to be easy. Modi knew it only too well.

Modi had hesitated over Vajpayee's offer, he said later, because he was out of touch with Gujarat politics, having been away in Delhi as the general secretary of the BJP in charge of a few state units like Himachal Pradesh. Soon Advani stepped in, and Modi heeded his advice. As his political mentor, Advani was fully aware of Modi's lack of administrative experience, but was very fond of him. Modi himself was aware of his lack of exposure – the quick transition from being a party organiser to the chief minister was no easy task. According to Modi's own disclosure, he had never been to the chief minister's office or the state legislative assembly before he was named CM. A similar occasion would occur thirteen years later, when Modi was elected the prime minister of India. He had never been to the Parliament House in Delhi before. One of the abiding images of Election 2014 will be that of Modi kneeling down to touch the steps leading up to the Central Hall of that grand edifice as he walked in to take oath as prime minister of the world's largest democracy. It was a great photo op, undoubtedly, but the gesture did have a ring of genuine humility.

When he was sworn in as chief minister of Gujarat on 7 October 2001, he had turned fifty-one only a few days earlier. He knew he faced the daunting task of cleaning up a mess he had inherited and braving the opposition from enemies within the BJP fold – who had sidelined him as early as 1992 and also from 1995 to 2001 from active state politics.

Then came the riots of February 2002.

In hindsight, many bring up the 2002 versus 1984 (anti-Sikh riots of 1984 instigated by some Congress leaders) argument. Writer-investigator Manoj Mitta had earlier co-written a book with HS Phoolka on the Delhi riots, titled *When a Tree Shook Delhi: The 1984 Carnage and its Aftermath*.[5] His title, of course, is taken from the notorious statement made by Rajiv Gandhi – referring to the violent reaction to the assassination of his mother Indira Gandhi by her Sikh security guards – that "when a big tree falls, the earth shakes". Political analysts aligned with the BJP often took comfort in comparing the fact that while in the Gujarat riots both Hindus and Muslims died, the anti-Sikh riots of 1984 were a one-sided affair. Besides, they also say, despite being an older case, almost all accused in the 1984 carnage have walked away with impunity while

many people have been sent to jail in the 2002 violence. It is no
secret that many Congress workers also took part in the 2002 riots
in Ahmedabad, hacking helpless Muslims to death.

Andy Marino has noted that by the evening of the second
day of the 2002 riots, no Congress leader from Gujarat had said
a word about the mindless violence. To Modi's credit, Marino says
he also found response to the Gujarat riots much swifter than
elsewhere: "Soldiers were deployed against rioters less than forty-
eight hours after Godhra and only twenty hours after the first death
in the ensuing communal violence. It was not ideal, but it was faster
than any other riot, and far sooner than any Congress administration
had previously managed. The riots in Bhagalpur in 1989, Hashimpura
in 1987, Surat in 1993 and Bombay in 1992 all went on for longer
and suffered higher death tolls than they should have as a result of
the Congress's dilatory attitude towards restoring order. In Delhi,
in 1984, no soldier was seen on the streets until the killings were
completely finished – four days after they began. "

Modi's plea to the people of Gujarat on 28 February 2002 through
Doordarshan to desist from violence and to control their emotions
evoked varied responses. His detractors say that by using the word
'cannibals', to refer to those allegedly responsible for burning the
railway coach of the Sabarmati Express, he was provoking Hindus
against the meat-eating Muslims – especially at a time when nobody
had any clue about the identity of those who committed the crime
and whether the attack was pre-planned or not. On the other camp,
there are those who argue that Modi categorically stated that a tit-for-
tat reaction was bad for Gujarat, which according to him, shouldn't
be made "to carry the burden of a black moment in history".

After attacking the perpetrators of the Godhra terror in the
strongest words possible, Modi appealed for calm: "I want to
express my gratitude to you in the midst of so much anger of the
18,000 villages of Gujarat. Only a few handfuls have experienced
disturbances. More or less, there has been an atmosphere of peace.
However, the development that has taken place in the cities of
Gujarat is disturbing... I am not here to give you advice or sermons.
But I can see the bright future of Gujarat and for that I have come

to seek your help. Come forward and help the government in the process of maintaining peace. The government seeks your help in the process of punishing the culprits through the legal route. The government seeks your help in creating the right atmosphere for this to happen. It is my faith that the people of Gujarat will respond to my feelings and together we shall work to ensure a peaceful Gujarat. That the innocent do not lose lives is our responsibility."

Now, Marino is not an exception and, in fact, there are many others – including those in the Congress party – who privately admit that Modi, a "small-town boy" new to administration, was a shaken man as the riots swept his state, and that he had appealed to the Centre and neighbouring states for help. Their response ranged from slow and tepid to cold, especially from Madhya Pradesh, then ruled by Digvijaya Singh of the Congress, who became one of Modi's wiliest critics. Modi's friends within the party claim that he wanted to resign as CM following the riots, but his party said no. It was Advani who groomed him inside the BJP and it was Advani who stood behind him like a pillar following public demand for sacking him as chief minister of Gujarat.

Perhaps it was the pride of a small-town man with loads of ambition that prompted Narendra Modi to interrupt then Prime Minister Vajpayee's reply to journalists in the immediate aftermath of the riots. Modi was never a favourite of Vajpayee. When a journalist asked Vajpayee what his message to the chief minister of Gujarat was, the BJP veteran responded with what appeared to be controlled displeasure – he said the chief minister should "follow his Rajdharma". He explained that Rajdharma is a meaningful term, and for somebody in a position of power, it meant not discriminating among the lower and the higher classes of society and people of any religion. In what seemed to be a bid to stop his senior from committing a faux pas, Modi turned towards Vajpayee on the dais, tried to catch his eye and said, "*Hum bhi wahi kar rahe hain, sahib* (that is what we are also doing, sir)." Vajpayee immediately changed tack and said, "I am sure Narendra*bhai* is also doing the same."

The defiance of Modi, the inscrutable politician driven by a voracious hunger for power and a relentless passion to extend his grip in Gujarat, was simple and total. That trait would play out many times over in the next decade that saw his ascent to the most powerful Indian leader of his time. And amid all concomitant *cris de coeur* for his prosecution, he wanted his side of the story to be heard, and his avowed plea to the media in the coming years was that he be subjected to rational critique, not witch-hunting through sensationalism and muckraking.

***

After the riots, all rats came out of the woodwork to bay for Modi's blood, a bureaucrat close to Modi told me angrily. The popular narrative woven by the electronic media and English-language newspapers has it that Modi connived with Hindu mobs that went on a killing spree in Muslim neighbourhoods in many parts of Gujarat. Volunteers of pro-Hindu militant outfits Vishwa Hindhu Parishad and Bajrang Dal have been caught on camera crowing about how they killed pregnant Muslim women, and men and children from the community. A *Tehelka* report in 2007 quoted Bajrang Dal leader Haresh Bhatt as saying that Modi had given them a free hand in rioting for three days after the Godhra train carnage. Bhatt said, "He (Modi) had given us three days... to do whatever we could. He said he would not give us time after that... He said this openly... After three days, he asked us to stop and everything came to a halt..." Bajrang Dal leader Babu Bajrangi told the *Tehelka* interviewer that after massacring Muslims in Naroda Patya, he felt like Maharana Pratap. "I'd heard stories about him but that day, I did what he did," he said.

Ten years after the riots, a special court awarded life terms to Maya Kodnani, BJP leader and former minister in Modi's cabinet, and Babu Bajrangi in the Naroda Patiya massacre case.

For his part, Modi and his lawyers denied any wrongdoing, and he has been cleared thrice by the courts as investigators could not establish his complicity in the riots. But for more than a decade, Modi operated in the shadow of doubt and in the process remained a much-maligned leader. The UK and US both revoked his visa, and he was a persona non grata in many countries in the West. While the BJP alleged a witch-hunt by the Congress-led alliance that was in power for a decade after forming the government in 2004, Manoj Mitta has argued that there are enough gaps in the inquiry done by the special-investigation team (SIT) led by senior police officer RK Raghavan, who, he argues in his book, *The Fiction of Fact-Finding: Modi & Godhra, a Study of the Gujarat 2002 Investigations*,[6] was unsuitable to head such a probe. In an interview to *Firstpost*, Mitta regrets that a person who conducted a shoddy probe into former Prime Minister Rajiv Gandhi's assassination at the hands of Sri Lanka Tamil terrorists unwittingly headed another shoddy probe, this time into Modi's alleged complicity in the 2002 carnage.

Mitta trains his guns on Raghavan in the *Firstpost* interview: "Raghavan was among the three police officers to have been indicted by the Verma Commission for security lapses leading to the assassination. Suicide bomber Dhanu was found to have been waiting for the former prime minister in the sterile zone long before his arrival. But, as the officer in charge of security at the fateful Sriperumbudur meeting (near Chennai on 21 May 1991), Raghavan claimed in a sworn statement that Dhanu had gate-crashed into the sterile zone only after Rajiv's arrival, that too because the VIP had himself beckoned to the people standing behind the police cordon. The Verma Commission diluted the finding against Raghavan by glossing over his affidavit. This allowed the Vajpayee government to resurrect his career in 1999 by appointing him CBI chief. The resurrection in turn allowed the Supreme Court to choose Raghavan for this vital post-retirement assignment as SIT chief. Had his affidavit been expressly discussed by the Verma Commission, it is unlikely that Raghavan would have been elevated to the CBI post, much less so entrusted with the politically sensitive responsibility of the Gujarat investigations."

***

Trammelled by the media, Modi, new to the ways of power politics, was initially fidgety about bad press in the aftermath of the 2002 riots though he won a state election by a landslide the same year. But he would soon learn that courting the media wasn't the only way to enhance his appeal and winnability. "He used to be angry about media interviews ending up a disaster in the beginning. But soon he picked up ways to deal with it," says a person who was closely associated with the image overhaul of Modi. The chief minister realised that using the wheels of time to his advantage required not being fast and first but being resilient. "He learnt from mistakes – such as the meaninglessness of blowing his top when he got very negative publicity. He chose to deal with the media indirectly, especially the vernacular media," this person told me.

The strategy was simple, says a person involved in the exercise. A team of publicists would go through reports in Gujarati dailies to look for negative news that needed government intervention. For example, there was once a report in a newspaper that a particular school didn't have roofs. The chief minister's office immediately instructed the public works department to look into the matter, and as soon as reparative measures were done, the newspaper editor was informed of the government action. The CMO would also thank the editors for publishing such stories and bringing to its attention pressing issues that called for government help.

"This began to click well," says the person.

Still under sharp attack in the electronic media and in English-language publications whenever a mention of the 2002 riots came up, Modi began instead to court religious sects, businessmen, opinion leaders, spiritual gurus and various others to go around the traditional media, to make new friends and drum up support for his widely publicised development initiatives in the state. He used the cold shoulder he received from Western nations as an opportunity to look to the East, and to learn the nuances of development from nations such as China, Japan and Korea.

In 2003, within months of a stunning poll victory in the state, he launched a drive to win over businesses, both local and overseas ones who had faced the heat during the riots and were hesitant to make further investments in Gujarat. *Caravan* magazine had reported that more than 1,000 trucks were set afire, a shipment of cars by General Motors torched and several businesses looted, resulting in a loss of more than Rs 2,000 crore for the industry on account of the riots – which meant that the dearth of goodwill from the industry was enormous. Several captains of industry had already made statements against Modi for not protecting minorities in the state. The likes of Deepak Parekh of Housing Development Finance Corporation (HDFC), NR Narayana Murti of Infosys Ltd. and so on were highly critical of Modi soon after the riots. At a Confederation of Indian Industry (CII) meet in Delhi in 2003, Modi was asked some tough questions about the business-friendliness and safety of doing business in Gujarat. Parsi businessmen were at the forefront of the attack. When Anu Aga of Thermax was at the helm of CII, it is rumoured that at the lobby group's lavish boat parties, members used to sing parodies, poking fun at Modi.

Modi plotted his revenge by engaging local businessmen actively in efforts to attract investments to the state. He got Gujarati businessmen – like Gautam Adani and others – to threaten the CII that a parallel forum would be floated in Gujarat, something that would jeopardise the national organisation's powers as a lobby. CII would be seen as a grouping without the support of rich Gujarati businessmen. CII didn't want to take the risk, especially when the NDA was in power. The BJP-led government had already begun to restrict access to CII, apparently for its stiff opposition to Modi. CII began to change its collective mind about Modi.

In 2003, one of the Gujarati businessmen came up with the idea of holding a summit to showcase the state as an investment destination. Thus was born the Vibrant Gujarat extravaganza. In the initial years, it saw Gujarati businessmen sponsor the event, but soon the government began to run the biennial show on its own by setting up a state-run organisation called iNDEXTb comprising senior state officials and former bureaucrats, among others. By 2010, the Gujarat government roped in American PR firm APCO Worldwide to manage the summit. *The Economic Times* reported that by 2011, the event drew investments in excess of Rs 20,000 crore despite the cascading effects of a global slowdown. By 2013 – Modi had been re-elected chief minister thrice by then, in 2002, 2007 and 2012 – the event, with its pomp and show, had begun to attract global attention and several MNCs and Indian industry bigwigs such as Ratan Tata, Mukesh Ambani, Sunil Mittal, Anil Ambani and Kumar Mangalam Birla became regular fixtures at the meet, notwithstanding any earlier antagonism towards Modi. From a business meet that just had the presence of Gujarat-based businessmen in 2005, in 2013, a total of 2,100 delegates from 121 countries attended the jamboree in which more than 2,500 business deals were signed for doing business in the western Indian state.

By then, Modi had become a darling of the Indian industry that had once despised and denigrated him. As mentioned in the previous chapter, Tata relocated its car plant business from Singur in West Bengal – where violent protests had forced the company to shut shop – to Gujarat. Though then chairman Ratan Tata had been averse to the idea of doing business in Gujarat after the riots, he did attend the Vibrant Gujarat summit in 2007, egged on by controversial PR head Niira Radia, who, it is said, told a reluctant Tata, "You should go there for my sake". The story has it that Modi then sent an SMS text to Ratan Tata in 2008, welcoming him to Gujarat to set up the plant to build cheap Nano cars. The Tatas were at that point scouting for land to relocate the Singur factory. Meticulous and zealous, Modi had already made arrangements to acquire land for the purpose if Ratan Tata said yes to his offer. It was such a sweet deal that no one could have refused, an official involved in the deal told me. A business leader like Ratan Tata endorsing the state was a shot in the arm for Modi.

More plaudits were to come. In 2009, Anil Ambani, quoting his late father Dhirubhai Ambani, called Modi a '*lambi race ka ghoda* (a long-distance runner)'. Modi also received copious praise from the likes of industrialist Sunil Mittal of the Bharti Group who extolled Modi's CEO-like qualities to run the country. Most of these businessmen also expressed their wish that the US revoke its ban on him entering that country. "It was a near impossible task from the point of view of changing the perception people had of him. Modi used all tools in his armoury to attract businessmen to the state, sops and lollies. Finally, he looked like a magician who had sold the idea of Gujarat's development to investors. There were gaps in MoUs getting materialised, but he sold them the idea very well nonetheless," an official who worked closely with Modi told me.

All was not so rosy within the BJP, however. With Modi's own growth in the ranks, he became his mentor Advani's biggest rival, resulting in the souring of ties between the two. Advani, assisted by the likes of Sushma Swaraj and others, went on to wage a prolonged battle since early 2013 within the party to stop Modi being named the spearhead for the party's 2014 Lok Sabha campaign and later as its prime ministerial candidate. Eventually, of course, Advani, Swaraj and all other Modi detractors had to yield. Similarly, most liberal intellectuals have never been able to come to terms with his rise. None other than Nobel Prize-winning economist Amartya Sen said that he would not like a person like Modi to be prime minister. His opinion of Modi perhaps summed up the intellectuals' distaste for the man. "I think I would like a more secular person to be prime minister. I would not like a prime minister who generates concern and fear on the part of minorities. That is the primary reason," he told me. And when Modi became PM, liberals, who should have ideally been happy to see a person from the working class rise to become the country's ruler, still held him in contempt – and it was mutual.

His was a dogged pursuit, but Modi, he of the narcissistic ways, always thought that he was destined to act and reign, and on his own terms.

Notes

1. Pub. Harvard University Press, 2009, US.
2. Pub. HarperCollins Publishers India, 2014, New Delhi.
3. The Emergency was imposed on 25 June 1975 after a high-profile political drama. It began with a case being filed by Indira Gandhi's opponent, Raj Narain, a leader from the Janata Party, in Allahabad High Court against Gandhi for election malpractices. Socialist leader Jayaprakash Narayan demanded her resignation when the court found her guilty on 12 June 1975 and declared her election to the Lok Sabha in 1971 void on the grounds of election malpractice. Gandhi challenged the verdict in the Supreme Court, which granted her a conditional stay. It allowed her to be a Member of Parliament but not preside over parliamentary proceedings. On 25 June, Narayan declared a nationwide plan of daily demonstrations in every state capital. The police, army and the people were asked to follow the Constitution rather than Indira Gandhi. The then President Fakhruddin Ali Ahmed

passed an ordinance about the state being in danger, and Emergency was imposed, giving Gandhi the power to rule by decree. All fundamental rights were suspended, politicians were arrested and heavy censorship was imposed on the media. It is regarded as the outcome of a systematic social, economic and political failure.

4. The then BJP President Murli Manohar Joshi had announced the "Ekta Yatra" (unity walk) from Kanyakumari in Kerala to Srinagar in Kashmir to hoist the tri-colour at Lal Chowk on 26 January 1992. The timing was significant. Kashmir was hit by militancy at this point and separatist leaders vowed to disrupt the yatra. They chalked out a joint strategy to stop BJP from raising the flag on the Srinagar clock tower. In anticipation of attack, the army and Border Security Force were deployed in Srinagar and a curfew imposed in the city. Several people were killed, including senior police officers, and many others injured by 26 January that year. The twelve-minute flag-hoisting ceremony itself saw tense moments as the flag broke into two and gunshots rang in the air. It was eventually remembered by Kashmiris as the moment when various militant factions came together against the state – unity of an unintended kind.

5. Pub. Roli Books, 2007, New Delhi.

6. Pub. HarperCollins Publishers India, 2014, New Delhi.

6 | OPPORTUNITY CALLING

"Politics is a lot of serendipity. You are in the right place and the right time and you've got the right message, and it either connects for you or, or it doesn't."

– Jon Huntsman Jr, American politician

When a frail old man sat down on a fast-unto-death *dharna* in front of Jantar Mantar in the scorching April of 2011, demanding an all-powerful anti-corruption ombudsman, it seemed like any other civic protest that Delhi's oldest astronomical observatory had watched over through decades. But soon, it turned out to be the launch of one of the biggest-ever protests in the history of free India.

Jantar Mantar, the unofficial protest venue in the national capital, could not hold the crowds of supporters that swelled each day. Not surprisingly, the second round of the fast – which took place in mid-August that year – was shifted some less than four kilometres away, to the sprawling Ramlila Maidan, which has a long history of hosting landmark events. Pandit Jawaharlal Nehru and Sardar Vallabhbhai Patel had organised meetings here during India's Independence struggle. In June 1975, it was the venue for Jayaprakash Narayan's one lakh-strong rally that rattled then Prime Minister Indira Gandhi who shortly imposed Emergency rule. After the Emergency was lifted and elections held, it was here that the triumphant opposition leaders who made history by routing Indira Gandhi's Congress in 1977 returned to celebrate their emphatic win. It was here that Anna

Hazare's protégé Arvind Kejriwal would take oath of office as chief minister of the state of Delhi, in a departure from the customary swearing-in at the Raj Bhavan, in December 2013.

Though he was a recipient of prestigious civilian awards such as the Padma Shri and Padma Bhushan as early as the 1990s, Kisan Baburao "Anna" Hazare was virtually unknown to most Indians until the summer of 2011 when he went on a hunger strike at Jantar Mantar as part of his India Against Corruption (IAC) strike. His emergence as a force to reckon with in mainstream politics was destined to have an enormous influence in the national elections that took place three years later. It exposed the self-serving motives of the ruling coalition, triggered renewed interest in politics, gave vent to the frustrated aspirations of the people, and inspired them to search for alternative leaders – playing them nicely into the hands of the BJP and its prime ministerial candidate Modi.

Hazare's fast started on 5 April and ended on 9 April 2011, a day after the government accepted his demands. The UPA government at the Centre – then led by Prime Minister Manmohan Singh and steered by powerful Congress President Sonia Gandhi – issued a gazette notification on the formation of a joint committee, consisting of government and civil society representatives, to draft the legislation. But when the government went back on its promise and came out with a softer law that didn't cover the prime minister's office and several others in its ambit, Hazare went on a fast yet again in the August of 2011, this time at Ramlila Maidan. He ended his fast on the thirteenth day, on 28 August, after the Indian Parliament decided to refer three of his demands (a citizen's charter, inclusion of lower bureaucracy and creation of Lokayuktas through a Lokpal Bill) to a parliamentary standing committee's consideration. By this time, a powerful new element in national politics had taken sudden birth. It was a surge of steadfast faith in the power of do-gooders who could shake the Central government.

The key takeaway from the unexpected success of IAC's campaign in swinging public opinion against a federal government was the dissemination of information about the protests and the creation of a political discourse around it. New media dominated conventional media in these aspects. Of course, the presence of spiritual gurus like Baba Ramadev chipping in with theatrics and drama further helped in attracting public attention, and TV channels happily went the whole hog with 24x7 coverage. Yet it was social media and cellphones that were pivotal to communicating with supporters across the national capital and beyond. The IAC agitation was, without an iota of doubt, a huge setback for the image of the UPA government that, up till then, looked irreplaceable for lack of an alternative. The main opposition, BJP, at that time was organisationally weak and undecided about a spearhead to take on a Congress-led coalition.

The IAC campaign, where door-to-door meetings were paramount, focused on highlighting the pitfalls and misdeeds of the government in power. Many senior ministers, including Kapil Sibal, Salman Khurshid, P Chidambaram, and other Congress leaders underestimated the nature of the challenge posed by IAC. In mid-August, the government arrested and lodged Hazare in jail, a move that proved to be very costly for the ruling dispensation because the anti-corruption leader's incarceration gave IAC the impetus to hit the road running. In response to their call, through emails and phone messages, thousands thronged city squares across the country as a mark of solidarity with Hazare. The event even captured newspaper headlines abroad – Hazare was named one of *Time* magazine's most influential persons of 2011. After he was released, the Gandhian activist's popularity and acceptability surged among urban middle classes, who, reeling from spiralling food prices and a sluggish economy, craved for change and were only too glad to put the blame for all the economic woes at the doors of the UPA.

This also meant that any attack on Hazare boomeranged and had people marching to the homes of ministers to register their protest and seek an apology. Congress spokesperson Manish Tewari had to retract a rather preposterous and unwarranted statement accusing Hazare of being corrupt from "head to toe". In the face of public outburst against his comments, Tewari disappeared from TV screens for several days and when he returned ten days later, he was forced to tender a public apology for his remark.

***

At the height of the Anna agitation in 2011, I stood in the dusty Ramlila grounds, where crowds jostled amiably and enthusiastic young men called out slogans on numerous microphones. Entire families had converged from across neighbouring states, many wearing white caps and T-shirts with the slogan 'I am Anna' or else wet hand-towels on their heads to keep them cool in the blaring summer sun. Traffic had come to a chaotic halt. Volunteers distributed *samosas, puri-bhaji* and syrupy-sweet glasses of tea with a picnic spirit. The mood was anarchistic. I asked a senior IAC leader, "Who manages your social media sites and bulk texting?"

"We have some teams helping us," he replied, without elaborating. Later, a Congress leader complained bitterly to me that a "foreign hand" was involved.

The "foreign hand" was Avaaz.org, an organisation that promotes pro-democracy movements through the Internet, social media, phones and sometimes with the help of citizen journalists. Avaaz was co-founded in 2007 by Res Publica, a global civic advocacy group, and Moveon.org, an online community for Internet advocacy in the US. The founding team had social entrepreneurs from six countries, including president and executive director Ricken Patel, Tom Perriello, Tom Pravda, Eli Pariser, Andrea Woodhouse, Jeremy Heimans, and David Madden. By 2011, Avaaz had run a total of 750 pro-democracy campaigns worldwide. Widely regarded as the largest global political web movement in history, Avaaz's website is blocked in China and Iran. One of its most victorious campaigns in a democracy was in Brazil, where it spearheaded the 2010 Ficha Limpa (clean record law) campaign that barred politicians with a criminal record from running for office. In fact, Patel told me he derived a lot of energy from the teachings of Mahatma Gandhi, who was the great source of inspiration of IAC and its leader Hazare. His favourite quote by the Mahatma was: "I am a human being first and a citizen of my country second".

Others besides the Congress who hated the activist group at that time included the regimes of Hosni Mubarak of Egypt, Muammar Gaddafi of Libya, Tunisia's Zine El Abidine Ben Ali and a host of others across the region that was later swept by the Arab Spring.

According to Patel, during Hazare's fast protest in 2011, first in April and later in August, two members joined Avaaz every second to express solidarity with Hazare's cause – to weed out corruption at all levels of the government. Patel told me in the September of 2011 that Avaaz raised funds through members for campaigns across the Middle East and in India and even in countries such as Brazil. They had a cap of USD 5,000 for individual donations, but still raised USD 500,000 a month.

In India, Avaaz's work included sending across press releases to a large number of email IDs of metro dwellers (collected through various agencies), bulk SMSes, organising media interactions, ads, and so on, explained Shivendra Singh Chauhan, the India representative of Avaaz. "I worked with Team Anna throughout the (2011) campaigns," he said.

When I broke the story for *The Economic Times*, IAC found the disclosure by Avaaz disconcerting, perhaps for fear of rivals raising the "foreign hand" question. But in hindsight, 2011 marked the entry of pros in India's campaign scene like never before, as political entrepreneurship began to gain momentum. In another year, by November 2012, IAC would break into two factions – those who favoured launching a political party and those who didn't. Arvind Kejriwal and others floated the Aam Aadmi Party (AAP) and for the first time, people without any prior experience could join politics, triggering a culture of political entrepreneurship among urban Indians. Hazare didn't approve.

The efforts of professionally run organisations like Avaaz.org would be replicated later in the general elections of 2014. While Avaaz worked in India through its eight lakh volunteers who emailed, SMSed and called up people on their phones to drum up support for Hazare in his fast-unto-death agitation demanding a stringent law to punish corrupt officials, brainiacs from IITs and Western universities who invaded the poll backrooms a few years later to throw their weight behind Narendra Modi's campaign would crunch numbers, demystify charts, bring in state-of-the-art electioneering technology to grassroots, unleash the latent power of the social media to the prime ministerial candidate's favour and collaborate with the RSS to map the route to poll triumph.

In retrospect, it was the Anna agitation that triggered an overwhelming anti-Congress sentiment across the country – it was tempting low-hanging fruit for any opposition party. The anti-corruption movement helped create a notion that the people of the country were living in a period of extreme lack of productivity, and that the government of the day, rattling under a raft of corruption charges and alleged abusive practices that perpetuated corporate oligarchy, had to go. The popular whine led to a faux Arab Spring movement in India's cities, especially in Delhi where the turnout at Hazare's agitations was huge. It began to dent the image of the Manmohan Singh government sputtering under heavy loads of scams, scandals and most importantly, slow economic growth and accelerating inflation.

By November 2012, when Hazare's lieutenant Arvind Kejriwal snapped his ties with IAC and his mentor to launch AAP, anger on the streets was palpable. By then, Kejriwal and his comrades had emerged as popular icons of the anti-corruption movement with a good following in the national capital. He and his band of *jholawalas* soon unleashed a campaign that forced the people to think that the government of the day was playing dice with their money, aspirations and their future.

***

But it was not the steely-minded Hazare or the dogged Kejriwal who alone unsettled the government of the day. The Congress by then had dug its own grave. At the time of the anti-graft protests, the government of Manmohan Singh had already been tainted by the cash-for-vote scam, Adarsh Housing Society scam, and the Commonwealth Games (CWG) scandal. More were yet to emerge.

The loss of face over the cash-for-votes scandal – which allegedly involved payment of bribes to BJP members of Parliament in return for abstention in a crucial vote on whether or not to pursue an India-US nuclear deal – was a blot on the government despite its poll win of 2009. The vote was necessitated by the 2008 withdrawal of support to the first UPA alliance by Left parties, which had offered an outside support to keep the Congress-led coalition in power. Though the government survived the 22 July 2008 vote, it earned a bad name after three BJP leaders stood up in Parliament and waved bundles of cash they claimed were paid to them by the Congress.

By 2010, within a year of it assuming office for the second straight term, the Manmohan Singh government was hurtling from crisis to crisis. It was in a soup over over-invoicing for projects and violation of labour laws. The Central Vigilance Commission, the official entity that looks into instances of governmental corruption, said in a report that there were irregularities in up to fourteen CWG projects. Soon, the government was rocked by the Adarsh Housing Society scam that saw senior military officers and bureaucrats bending rules to annex property and land allotted to war widows and defence officials in a plush, 31-storey building constructed in the tony neighbourhood of Colaba in Mumbai. The Congress chief minister of Maharashtra, Ashok Chavan, had to step down from the post after the scam was unearthed in November 2010.

The next year, the Comptroller and Auditor General of India, the country's internal auditor, dropped a bombshell by declaring that India had incurred a loss of more than Rs 1.7 trillion thanks to politicians and government officials undercharging mobile telephony companies for frequency-allocation licenses. This new scandal involved the allocation of 122 second-generation airwaves across the country's twenty-two telecom zones. These licences were meant to create 2G subscriptions for cellphones. Licences were given to telecom companies in 2008 at a price arrived at in 2001 and on a first-come-first-serve basis. However, the then telecom minister Andimuthu Raja was accused of accepting Rs 3,000 crore from interested companies in return for advancing the cut-off date for applications for spectrum allocation to 25 September from 1 October 2007, which amounted to subverting the government's first-come-first-serve policy. After the wheeling-dealing was unearthed, A Raja had to step down and face a probe, and many of his accomplices were kept in judicial custody in Delhi's Tihar jail for many months. The UPA government would come under a cloud over several more deals. Manmohan Singh was directly in charge of the coal ministry and has come under repeated charges of presiding over the worst era in coal corruption.

Less than a year after the 2G scam uproar, and weeks after the formation of AAP, India was wracked by a tragedy of a more personal kind.

On 16 December 2012, a 23-year-old physiotherapy student was gang-raped and brutalised while travelling in an empty public bus in Delhi, returning home after watching a movie, *Life of Pi*, with a male friend. Born to a lower-middle-class family, the young woman had a promising career and life ahead of her and was the apple of the eye of her father, who sold his agricultural land to pay for her education. Attacked by a group of six men – who used steel rods to pierce the girl's genitals and pull out her intestines – her screams for help went unheeded on the noisy streets of south Delhi as the bus sped about with shut tinted windows. She was later thrown out of the bus, naked and fatally wounded, along with her friend, who had also been beaten up and his bones broken. The two lay semi-conscious by the side of a cold, crowded road, ignored by passers-by who did not wish to get their hands dirty in what was obviously a scene of heinous crime.

The two were taken to a government hospital by the police where the girl was put on life support but her condition deteriorated daily. By 19 December, most of her remaining intestines had been surgically removed, and she was able to give her statement to the police. But her fever continued to rise. On 26 December, a Cabinet meeting chaired by Manmohan Singh decided to fly the girl to a multi-organ transplant speciality hospital in Singapore. She had a cardiac arrest on the flight and did not regain consciousness in Singapore. She died on 29 December and was flown back to Delhi for a high-security cremation on 30 December.

Using the couple's statements along with evidence from CCTV cameras and other sources, the police was able to nab all six criminals, mostly migrants from the impoverished villages of the country's Hindi belt, within twenty-four hours and put the case on a 'fast track' so as to convict them in the least possible time.[1]

They had to. For by then, India had erupted in a bomb of outrage.

Public anger had simmered while news of the assault spread and the government appeared to be asleep. It finally burst into furious protests on 21 December on Rajpath at the doorstep of Rashtrapati Bhavan, the presidential palace, where young men and women showed up brandishing their middle fingers at the haloed walls above them, screaming for justice.

At every step and at every turn from then on, the government dug itself deeper and deeper into a cesspit of unpardonable apathy and shame. Protestors – including college students, young children and senior citizens – were beaten up, *lathi*-charged and water-hosed, day after day, protest after protest. Seven metro stations were arbitrarily shut down to prevent people from collecting in the central Delhi area, leaving lakhs of daily commuters helpless and throwing city life out of gear. Rahul Gandhi, the new face of the Congress that was attempting a youthful overhaul, was completely missing in action. Sheila Dikshit, Delhi's chief minister and Congress leader, also stayed behind doors, saying she did not have the "courage to face the victim's family". President Pranab Mukherjee's son Abhijit Mukherjee called some of the protesters 'dented-painted women' in a grotesquely misplaced attempt at undermining their cause. Home Minister Sushil Shinde further went and put his foot in his mouth, saying, "If we meet students today, tomorrow we may have to meet Maoists," comparing the student-led agitation to the Naxal insurgency. Finally, Sonia Gandhi had to step in and instruct Shinde to take quick action to solve the matter.

The government tried conventional ways of tackling the situation. Sonia Gandhi belatedly visited the girl's bereaved family. The prime minister made an unemotional speech on television comparing the victim to his three daughters – a telecast that was rubbished as mechanised and a matter of 'too little, too late'. This was an extreme situation that required lightning-quick, effective measures but the government in power fell short. Needless to say, it was a public-relations horror. The international media ran provocative images of peaceful protestors being beaten up by police, slogans shouting bitterly, "Rape is okay but protesting against rape is not okay". Headlines declared Delhi the 'rape capital' of the world. Cities across India caught the fever of public fury and protests spread like wildfire. Women's groups demanded stricter anti-rape laws. Schools and colleges held *dharnas* and candle-light vigils. It was a rude awakening for the common man and woman on the street, who suddenly realised they were not safe and their government didn't seem to care. Coming so soon at the heels of major political and financial scams, the Congress's poor response to the 2012 gang-rape was yet another nail in their coffin.

The taint on the Congress was to be manna for Modi.

***

For a coalition that had the advantage of ruling India when the global economy grew at a faster clip and the disadvantage of being in power when powerful national economies started shrinking, UPA was lucky in the beginning and unlucky later. In emerging economies such as India and China, the impact of the 2008 slowdown that devastated Western markets wasn't palpable even in 2009 when the UPA was re-elected on the back of its welfare policies and an all-round growth.

The effect was delayed for obvious reasons: economies such as India and China didn't have too much of an exposure to the global financial shock. These countries had many restrictions on international capital inflows. Harvard University professor Gita Gopinath has succinctly explained the global scenario of the time: "Domestic financial intermediation is more heavily regulated in India. The crisis in the US market was due to esoteric financial instruments like credit default swaps and the high leverage that the unregulated non-banking financial institutions took on. These factors were not important in India and China. Of course, this does not mean that India and China have a better financial system. In both countries there is large scope for improving the financial system," she said.

Eventually, however, the effects of the global meltdown did catch up with India and China as well. By 2010, when the full impact of the worldwide slowdown finally began affecting the Indian economy, the country was home to large numbers of people who had managed to earn and make a living without government handouts. But the UPA government's focus was not them, and the regime would pay dearly for ignoring this new group of aspiring classes who had just begun to enjoy their freedom of living without entitlements. Their story goes back a couple of decades. As Columbia University professor and renowned economist Arvind Panagariya points out, India had slid into slow growth as well as slow progress in education and health thanks to the command-and-control system prior to 1991. The effects of liberalisation produced verifiable results. He explains, "Growth accelerated and social spending rose as well... On the one hand, rapid growth directly empowers the citizens through increased incomes that they can use to buy high-quality education and health in the marketplace. On the other hand, it gives the government ever-rising revenues to further enhance public expenditures on health and education." As entrepreneurship flourished, jobs rose and more people found their way out of abject poverty and dependence on the security offered by official schemes for the poor. Poverty in India declined to a record 22 percent in 2011-12, according to the country's Planning Commission. Over a decade, from 2001-02 to 2011-12, poverty witnessed a consistent decline with the levels dropping from 37.2 percent in 2004-05 to 29.8 percent in 2009-10. Many economists argue that this was due to the trickle-down effect of high growth.

It wasn't surprising that the priorities of the UPA were different from those of the three successive governments from 1991 to 2004. Those three governments of different political hues were busy liberalising the economy. Renowned economist Jagdish Bhagwati has argued that the growth in the initial years of the UPA was thanks to a robust global economy and the policies pursued by powerful prime ministers during 1991 to 2004.

Bhagwati had explained to me in an interview in late 2012 that Manmohan Singh's hands were tied by the peculiar nature of governance in place, referring to remote controlling of the running of his government by Congress president Sonia Gandhi. Bhagwati went to the extent of comparing the Singh government to the former Soviet system where the communist party was supreme and the chief of government was just a figurehead. "His (Singh's) ability to deliver reforms is handicapped by the fact that the people in favour of track-II reforms (social spending, et cetera) around Ms Gandhi are not appreciative of the fact that track-I reforms (growth-oriented initiatives) are absolutely necessary, that we need to intensify and broaden them to continue making a direct impact on poverty and generating revenues (for welfare schemes)," Bhagwati had told me in an interview. He was very critical of economists who had lauded Singh's policies. "A lot of them (even luminaries such as Amartya Sen and Mahbub ul Haq) used to say that growth wouldn't influence poverty. Now, it is clear that growth did influence poverty. And they did shift their arguments continuously... (those economists) are like New York's cockroaches. You can't wipe them out. They will turn up perennially," Bhagwati said, claiming that he stood vindicated in his position that redistribution alone cannot make a big impact in bringing down poverty.

Under Singh, expenditure and economic activity started shrinking. Employment generation, too, was slow. So was growth in manufacturing, which fell in several quarters in the last years of the UPA-II. Without doubt, the institution of the PMO had lost its lustre under Singh as he waited for instructions from Sonia Gandhi. The role of the prime minister has been crucial for reforms. This was evident in the case of Narasimha Rao in 1991-1996 and AB Vajpayee in 1998-2004. But by 2011-12, the National Advisory Council (NAC), headed by Sonia Gandhi, had become an alternative power centre that was more powerful than the PMO. The casualty, of course, was governance.

The low-profile Manmohan Singh would also never put his foot down when powerful Cabinet colleagues thrust indiscreet policies upon the government. The move to tax overseas companies for transactions that they had entered into in India in the past also shattered investor confidence in the Indian economy. One of the companies under the radar was the biggest foreign corporate investor in India, Vodafone. The tax department sent Vodafone a tax bill of Rs 3,200 crore for allegedly undervaluing the shares Vodafone issued to its parent company. The tax department said that this difference in valuation was in fact a disguised loan subject to transfer pricing provisions. Vodafone argued that share premium is a capital receipt, not income and hence not taxable. The case stretched on so long, it scared off potential overseas investors.

શાળાની જુ. ડિ. એન.સી.સી.ની એક રૂપ

Young Narendra was an NCC cadet. This 1965 photo from the archives of the Bhagavatacharya Narayanacharya High School shows a 15-year-old Modi seated first from right (second row from below).

Modi incognito (dressed as a Sikh) to evade arrest during the Emergency imposed by the Prime Minister Indira Gandhi, who suspended civil liberties and threw many opposition leaders in jail.

Modi at an RSS function. He was associated with the Hindu umbrella organisation when he was in school and formally joined it when he was twenty-one.

Modi with former Gujarat chief minister Keshubhai Patel and RSS functionaries.

Modi with former Prime Minister Atal Bihari Vajpayee.

Columbia university professor Arvind Panagariya (above) and his mentor Jagdish Bhagwati, both celebrated economists, have lauded Modi for his development initiatives.

Modi with his one-time mentor LK Advani, who would later lose out to him in the race for prime ministership.

Modi with his mother Hiraben.

Modi's estranged wife Jashodaben, a retired school teacher who lives in the Mehsana district of Gujarat. A few months after his becoming the PM, she filed an RTI seeking details of the order that had assigned her a security entourage. She felt threatened by the presence of armed guards following her every move in air-conditioned vehicles while she used public transport. She was denied information under RTI.

Actor Salman Khan with Modi. Khan told a news channel that the BJP heavyweight need not apologize for the Gujarat riots since the courts had given him a clean chit.

Modi with his right-hand man and BJP president, Amit Shah.

This page and facing: Modi had laid great emphasis on campaign through social media; in the run-up to the polls, his campaign managers unleashed a blitzkrieg lapping him up as a doer who alone could put India on the fast-track of growth.

You Tube   janta maaf nahi karegi ad

BJP Hindi TVC - Janata Maaf Nahi Karegi

Bharatiya Janata Party

 76,001

18,246

+ Add to   < Share   ••• More   195   36

India First   ₹ 199.00   Namo For PM   ₹ 199.00   Nation First   ₹ 199.00

Social Icon   ₹ 249.00   Nation First   ₹ 249.00   Calligram   ₹ 349.00

OUT OF STOCK

Apparel
T- Shirt, Koti

Mug
Coffee-Mug

Stationery
Notebook, Desk Organizers

Tech
Pen Drive

POPULAR PRODUCTS

Above, below, and facing page: An array of Modi merchandise was released during the 2014 election campaign, akin to US-style political campaigning and sport extravaganzas worldwide.

The second round of Modi's *Chai pe Charcha* campaign was held on Women's Day, 8 March 2014, with the theme of 'Women Safety and Empowerment'.

Above, below and facing page: The focus of the BJP's campaign was to hard sell Modi. His face was everywhere during the elections, from the front pages of dailies to the backs of auto rickshaws

Modi's massive rally on 24 April 2014, turned the holy town of Varanasi into a sea of saffron.

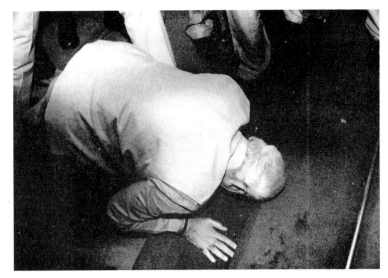

Modi entered the Indian Parliament as prime minister for the first time on 20 March 2014, the day the BJP parliamentary party nominated him for the post. He touched the steps of the Parliament with his forehead in an act of reverence.

Modi, the son of an impoverished tea seller from a tiny Gujarat town, took oath of office as prime minister of the world's largest democracy on 26 May 2014.

The UPA, which in its first term (2004 to 2009) was backed by Left parties and therefore put a lot of emphasis on social spending, exhibited no stark difference in its policy thrust when it returned to power in 2009 after snapping ties with the Left. Here was an opportunity to put the country back on the reform track. But consistent expansion of its key entitlement-focused schemes unveiled during the 2004-2009 period shrank space for fiscal management. Besides, after being besieged by a series of corruption scandals in the second term, the government ended up delaying and even stalling various big-ticket infrastructure and industrial projects aimed at kickstarting the growth momentum. Panagariya is of the view that "the paralysis with regards to decision-making in the UPA government" started with reluctance in giving clearances to such projects by the environment ministry under Jairam Ramesh first and then under Congress leader Jayanthi Natarajan, who faced unconfirmed charges of soliciting bribes for clearing projects. She had to finally step down from the ministerial post in early 2014 for, it appeared, delaying of projects for months without giving any plausible reason. By the time the seniors in the party took note and intervened, such criminal negligence of aborting new projects had done major damage to the Indian economy, already wobbling under the weight of deteriorating investor sentiment.

As a result of myriad such episodes that undermined the prime minister's authority, the investment climate in the country was hurt by misplaced priorities of the government. Coupled with a sharp slide in growth and fall in job creation, the UPA, in its late phase, symbolised waning momentum in economic growth. Its welfare policies became a burden and an additional risk for the Singh government grappling with spiralling inflation, depreciation of the rupee, widening current account deficit and numerous other fiscal constraints. According to pundits, the case brought to the fore the UPA government's reluctance to get rid of unpredictable rules and regulations in the country. When Manmohan Singh's government had taken charge in 2004, the country's economy was growing at a robust 8.1 percent – it grew even faster over the next few years until early 2008, posting more than 9 percent growth for three straight years. But by 2013, the economy was growing at its slowest pace in more than a decade – 4.5 percent. On the job front, too, achievements were modest.

A paper published in late 2013 by the Institute of Applied Manpower Research (IAMR), a think-tank of the Planning Commission, titled, 'Joblessness and Informalization: Challenges to Inclusive Growth in India', revealed the enormity of jobless growth during the UPA's second term. The report blamed the Centre for pushing millions to become casual labour with little social security. The report noted that fifteen million workers shifted out of agriculture and into the manufacturing and services sector during 2005-10, leading to agriculture's share in total employment falling from 57 percent to 53 percent. In the same period, the construction sector added eighteen million people as workers as the government made huge investments in infrastructure. "Out of forty-four million total employment in construction by 2010, forty-two million (informal labour) hardly have any kind of social security benefit attached with it. In other words, 95 percent of workers in construction sector hardly have any kind of social security coverage," the study added, and warned that a "daunting and complicated task confronting the policymakers is to address the issue of informal employment within the organised sector. This issue of informalisation of employment poses a serious challenge in achieving decent work and thereby achieving more inclusive growth and sustainable development".

From 2005-10, the manufacturing sector saw the loss of five million jobs. The services sector, which had seen a massive growth during 2000-2005 of eighteen million jobs, witnessed only four million additional jobs in 2005-2010. "Undoubtedly, construction driven by significant expansion of infrastructure investment during the eleventh Five-Year Plan has helped in absorbing surplus workers from agriculture sector. However, ensuring decent employment for those moving out of agriculture remains a big challenge," the report said. It highlighted the worrying fact that the share of informal workers in the total workforce in India is well above other emerging market economies (93 percent of all workers compared to 55 percent in Brazil). The plight of India's workers coming out of agriculture got only worse later – from 2010 to 2014. In short, UPA ended up demoralising the middle classes driven by huge aspirations.

The Congress, for its part, had argued vehemently that its flagship scheme, Mahatma Gandhi National Rural Employment Generation Act (MGNREGA), was successful in offering jobs to the needy and to assure the sustenance of the poor. Development economists such as Jean Dreze and twenty-seven others argued in a joint statement that MGNREGA (popularly pronounced *en-rega*) provides employment to fifty million poor households at a low cost of 0.3 percent of the country's GDP. They also argue that the Rs 2.5 trillion the UPA spent from 2005 to the end of fiscal year ending March 2015 is nothing short of a huge success.

Whatever top economists may say, empirical evidence suggests that job schemes don't lead to rise in rural wages. Pro-MGNREGA economists didn't seem to look at the opportunity costs – gains that would have come if the money were channeled into building rural infrastructure; the rural poor often stand to gain from roads, water projects and sanitation. The scheme eventually led to poorer economic activity in the countryside with workers being assured of daily wages. After winning the 2014 elections, political opponents to MGNREGA in the new BJP government called it a "partisan plan", and the worst fears of the likes of Dreze would soon come true: "NREGA *marega* (NREGA would die)".

Many economists have also argued that cash transfers were the better option, and not assured jobs that make rural folk lazy and less productive. As stated earlier, many poor people who had managed to wriggle out of the entitlement bracket were looking for better job opportunities and infrastructure. They were deeply resentful of the Centre glibly doling out lollies, which instead led to shortage of labour and high costs of entrepreneurial activities. The disillusionment against the government led by Singh, the man who pioneered India's reforms, was on many fronts. He was the one who put his foot down on the issue of signing the India-US civil nuclear deal in 2008, but by 2010 American companies had started talking "India fatigue", referring to the lack of ease in doing business in India. The highlight of his rule was the passage of the Right to Information Act (RTI), which ironically, gave anti-corruption crusaders enough ammunition to target his own government over corruption scandals. Besides, the BJP's ruse to stall proceedings in the Lok Sabha for months on end gave traction to the argument that the UPA was neck-deep in policy paralysis. Evidently, with public perception tilted against the government of the day, Singh was the butt of attack for all the "inactivity" and the opposition managed to get away with the unsavoury move of disrupting the business of Parliament over the trivial justification of exercising their freedom to protest.

Finally, Modi was destined to tap popular frustration to a meaningful conclusion and to exploit the general disenchantment with Singh, who had the longest stint at the PMO after the first Prime Minister Jawaharlal Nehru's seventeen years in power.

***

The assembly elections of November 2013, especially in Madhya Pradesh, Rajasthan and Chhattisgarh, also dealt major setbacks to the Congress party, a forewarning of things to come. The GOP appeared tame in the run-up to the elections with its workers already demoralised. Many Congress workers I had met in Bhopal (ahead of the Madhya Pradesh elections) rued that the Congress leadership was not doing enough to stop the Modi bandwagon. "Modi is everywhere, where are our leaders?" a Mahila Congress leader wondered. Of course, Sonia Gandhi and Rahul Gandhi had campaigned tirelessly, addressing many rallies in states that went to the poll. But they seemed to be outsmarted by the BJP with its hi-tech campaign strategy.

The Congress was also fatigued thanks to the anti-incumbency wave that had transformed into a tsunami by the time the country went to the polls in April. While I was in central Uttar Pradesh during the height of the campaign, a Congress worker in Farrukhabad, which was then represented by Union minister Salman Khurshid who later lost in the polls, disclosed to me that he found it difficult to convince even traditional voters of the Congress why they should vote for the Congress in 2014. "I appealed even in the name of my religion, Islam, to a fellow Muslim to vote for Congress, but he said,

'The Congress can no longer stop Modi'. They were very unhappy with Rahul's amateur politics and the rot of dynasty that was on full display in the Congress," he said.

The rot that the Congress worker mentioned had set in long ago, but Rahul's bid to undermine the PMO over a range of issues ended up damaging his own prospects as a campaigner for the Congress in the 2014 elections.

Many Congress leaders in Delhi had backed Rahul in his amateurish antics (they all said later, in hindsight that he was wrong), including his act of publicly tearing into pieces an ordinance his own party had been trying to pass in government. The ordinance was meant to negate a Supreme Court order on disqualifying convicted MPs and MLAs. Rahul appeared out of nowhere at a September 2013 press conference at the Delhi Press Club where a Congress leader was holding forth about the ordinance. The Gandhi scion dramatically rolled up his sleeves, described the government's move as complete nonsense, and tore the ordinance to pieces as if he knew nothing of it until he walked into that meeting.

But that move, which according to calculations of a few Congress strategists, was meant to help Rahul distance himself from the UPA's omissions and commission, didn't click. On the other hand, it delivered a huge a blow to the image of the government and also that of his mother Sonia Gandhi who was part of the Congress core group meeting that had cleared the ordinance proposal in the first place.

"The gimmicks didn't work. The Congress by then was in disarray and was in bad light. Rahul's mannerisms and statements and interviews (some of which were disastrous; he appeared not to be answering the interviewer's questions but blurting out what he had learnt by heart) didn't help either," a senior Congress leader told me after the polls. He is of the view that Rahul did the right thing by not pitching himself against Modi as the PM candidate of the Congress, because he was anyway no match for the BJP heavyweight. "All the blame for the loss would have been on him," this leader added. Modi often pitched the same argument at public rallies, chiding the 'shehzaada' for being a coward.

The electorate read it as absolute reluctance on the part of the young Gandhi to take the plunge into a position of responsibility and power. The Congress itself was racked with conflict between Rahul's supporters and doubters, which led to an incoherent marketing strategy. The Congress team was just not able to popularise Rahul across social media the way Modi supporters did – on the contrary, Rahul was tagged 'Pappu' (informal name for a foolish, immature young boy) by opponents and scores of cartoons flooded Twitter and Facebook mocking his meekness and 'mama's boy' image. Rahul's bland press conferences and ambiguous answers to tough questions also contrasted badly with Modi's mature media savviness, brevity, sense of purpose and an air of intimidation. Later, with a series of unsettling reverses in the state polls after the general election, Rahul looked more lost than he was reluctant. To the man on the street, Rahul Gandhi was a washout.

***

Besides the BJP, Arvind Kejriwal's AAP was also seen as a contender to power. But to the BJP's relief, it was hobbled by inherent contradictions within a short period of time. Sumantra Bose, professor of international and comparative politics at the London School of Economics and Political Science, who has followed the trajectory of movements like AAP, both in the developed and the developing worlds, told me: "Usually, such efforts have not proved sustainable or successful."

He compared the anti-corruption Ficha Limpa protests in Brazil of 2010 with the Anna Hazare-led India Against Corruption movement of 2011. Both were triggered by public anger against the political establishment, and corruption emerged as one of the main issues. But there were differences, too. Bose argued the IAC, from which AAP was formed, had a better shelf-life than the Brazilian outburst. "The Brazilian protests subsided after a few weeks, and may go down as a 'one-off' flareup. The IAC agitation was much more organised. It was also far smaller, despite the media attention it drew. The Brazil events saw large demonstrations all over that country, involving several million people in dozens of cities and towns," Bose said, going on to emphasise that the AAP's appeal was fundamentally rooted in its "freshness" and in its strong, if vague, anti-status quo rhetoric and posturing. "It capitalised on the nearly pervasive sense of deep disappointment with the Centre's Congress-led government and its leadership," he noted.

Bose's contention that pro-people movements crumble in the absence of a centralised party apparatus has been proved right many times over. Civil-society movements that have tried to reinvent themselves as political parties have shared a similar fate. This phenomenon was noted with gusto by none other than Karl Marx himself. In his analysis of the formation and the fall of Paris Commune, a socialist government in France that lasted only seventy-two days in 1871, Marx attributed its failure to a highly "decentralised structure" of governance.

Historically, such efforts by civil society groups to cobble together a political entity have proved sustainable only when they replace decentralised entities with a centralised hierarchy – as seen in most political parties with longevity. The best example of such an overnight transformation is Russia after the October Revolution of 1917. Lenin, a skillful organiser and a Marx scholar, didn't want his regime to repeat the mistakes of Paris Commune. He brought in a strong and centralised party very similar to the hierarchy of the Catholic Church. His move – a rather drastic effort at implementing Marx's teachings – led to the near abolition of "soviets", or workers' councils, and the "Soviet Union" became a communist party dictatorship.

Certainly, it is naïve to compare Paris Commune, a nineteenth-century phenomenon, with a twenty-first-century one, the Aam Aadmi Party (AAP), which made a spectacular debut in the Delhi assembly polls of 2013, not only by winning twenty-eight seats in the seventy-member House, but also by decimating the incumbent Congress. Its leader Kejriwal was called a 'giant-slayer' when he defeated the then Chief Minister Sheila Dikshit in her traditional New Delhi assembly constituency, which she'd won for three successive terms. While AAP did well in Delhi's municipal area – Kejriwal's main staging post – it didn't make a mark in non-municipal (relatively rural) areas. In these outlying parts of the city-state, the

BJP secured over 14 percent more votes than AAP did. Besides, AAP, as pointed out by Pradeep Chhibber, political science professor at University of California, Berkeley, ended up hurting the Congress more, robbing Delhi's ruling party of its political agenda. Chhibber and colleagues Harsh Shah and Rahul Verma wrote in a column in *The Economic Times* just after the Delhi assembly elections, "The Congress's centrist narrative is being fundamentally challenged by the Aam Aadmi Party whose social and economic policies are closer to the Congress's platform than to any other party's. AAP is, however, promising to run a better, cleaner, and more responsive government. It has also positioned itself as the party of the people (at least in Delhi)."

They added, "At the same time, the BJP under Modi has clearly defined itself as the Right-wing alternative – economically and socially. This leaves the Congress with very little space to manoeuvre, except maybe to hand out more dole. The Congress may choose to adopt a set of populist policies in the hope of winning, but as long as those measures are implemented by a corrupt and inefficient administration, they will not and cannot be translated into votes."

However, AAP was beset by problems of its own, notably the lack of a centralised leadership, which came to the fore with AAP leaders making contradictory remarks over a range of issues from caste to alliance. "There is certainly a lack of strong party structure in AAP. Besides, its only agenda is to fight corruption. They are yet to come up with a 'vision' for their party," a communist leader told me.

AAP's win in Delhi was historic, but not an unprecedented phenomenon. The poll triumphs of charismatic actor NT Rama Rao of the Telegu Desam Party (TDP) in Andhra Pradesh 1983 and that of the Asom Gana Parishad in Assam 1985 were far more stunning. TDP was formed in 1982 and it swept to power within nine months of its formation in the 1983 assembly elections, winning 202 of the 294 seats, and securing more than 45 percent of the votes polled. The Congress had won only sixty seats then. Similarly, the Asom Gana Parishad (AGP), formed just two months before the Assam state election of 1985, won sixty-seven of the 126 seats.

AAP's Delhi Chief Minister Kejriwal also made some fundamental errors ahead of the 2014 general elections. Within forty-nine days of coming to power, he stepped down as chief minister citing his inability to get a strong anti-corruption bill passed in the Delhi assembly. He accused the BJP and Congress of ganging up against him to stall the bill. His resignation as CM came as a blow to common people who had voted him to power expecting that he would deliver. AAP also made the mistake of spreading out wide across the country to contest from 443 of the 543 seats in the country's general election, instead of focusing on urban centres where it had created a buzz. Kejriwal had become far too ambitious by then, pitting himself against Modi from the Varanasi seat, hoping to be a giant-slayer yet again.

But Kejriwal's retreat from the corridors of power in Delhi had done irreparable damage to his image in the eyes of Indian voters. If he could not lead a city, how would he lead a nation? Options of leaders diminished. Rahul Gandhi and Arvind Kejriwal were too raw to lead. India needed someone with the tenacity and grit to be in it for the long haul, no matter what his past.

When the idea of Modi dawned, India was ready and willing.

Notes

1. By 22 December 2012, all six accused in the 16 December 2012 bus gang-rape case had been arrested. On 3 January 2013, the police filed a charge-sheet against the five adult accused for murder, gang-rape, attempt to murder, kidnapping, unnatural offences, dacoity, et cetera. One of the six was proved to be a minor, hence he was tried separately. On 11 March, Ram Singh, one of the adult accused, committed suicide while in prison. The case was put through a special 'fast-track' court with three international news agencies given permission to cover it. On 31 August, the minor was convicted of gang-rape and murder, and sentenced to three years in a probation home, the maximum allowed under juvenile law. The remaining four were convicted on 13 September and were awarded the death sentence. Six months later, the High Court upheld the verdict. The four have currently appealed to the highest authority in the country, the Supreme Court, and have been granted a stay on their execution pending its verdict.

7 DIASPORA POWER

"The prime minister has the trust not only of Indians in India, but that of so many Non-Resident Indians and People of Indian Origin who believe in the promise of his leadership in India."

– Dr Bharat Barai, president of the Indian American Community Foundation, which organised Narendra Modi's mega public interaction at Madison Square Garden, New York, on 28 September 2014

It was a few days after the 2014 election results were announced and I was in the mood for Scandinavian salmon. On a wet, chilly morning in Finland's capital city – chilly by Indian standards, summer according to the Finns – I contentedly tucked into shallow-fried, freshly caught salmon served on a plastic plate in a makeshift yellow tent on the Helsinki waterfront, which at that time of the day was deserted except for fish vendors waiting for the next boat from the former military island of Suomenlinna, and albatrosses circling above and occasionally diving into the turbulent, icy sea. As I ate, a turbaned Indian appeared out of nowhere. Coming closer to me, he stared at my plateful of fish with an expression of disgust and asked, "From India?" This was no place to ignore a fellow Indian, especially not one in such a forlorn outpost. "Yes," I replied. He switched into Hindi with great ease, sought forgiveness for assuming I was from Pakistan (perhaps due to my carnivorous delight in the fish on my plate) and hugged me as congratulations for electing Narendra Modi to power. "Our country will now scale new heights," he said with gusto, and disclosed that he had been living in Helsinki for the past thirty years. A few minutes of conversation ensued, peppered with words like "Indianness", before the middle-aged Sardar*ji* shook my hands again in goodbye, and disappeared into the grey drizzle.

It was a similar sense of pride in Indianness that drove Atlanta, US-based Amitabh Sharma to fly into India on 4 February 2014 with the intent of doing what he calls "*seva* (service)". He would work for the next three months among the Dalits of central Uttar Pradesh to highlight Narendra Modi's "achievements" in Gujarat where Modi had been chief minister since late 2001. Sharma also ventured occasionally into villages and small towns where Muslims lived. His idea was to wean voters away from the grip of the Samajwadi Party (SP) and the Bahujan Samaj Party (BSP). He felt that SP leader Mulayam Singh had created a dynasty and that had to be dismantled; the BSP, on its part, had successfully wooed Dalits and offered them nothing in return while its leader Mayawati amassed a lot of wealth. "I wanted to tell them about the option they had in uplifting themselves out of abject poverty: that is to vote for Modi who has done wonders in Gujarat," says Sharma, a 61-year-old chief executive and founder of a software company, Asterix Solutions. Born in Agra, Sharma worked in the software business in India before shifting base to Atlanta in 1995, where he set up the World Hindu Organisation in 2013. The Kurukshetra University-alumnus had been closely associated with various other Hindu organisations in the US, many of whom have campaigned zealously for Narendra Modi.

Sharma spent almost eight hours a day visiting Dalit families across constituencies like Saharanpur, Mainpuri, Etawah, Firozabad and others. Armed with his laptop and his clearly "NRI appearance", Sharma would walk into poor households in these regions and strike up conversations with a group of men and women before giving them a "class" on the Gujarat model of development. He would show them videos and pictures of the Sabarmati riverfront, one of Modi's showpiece projects, and those of the public transport network in Ahmedabad. He would engage them in debates about the benefits of having Modi as prime minister. He realised that people were wonderstruck by an Indian residing in the US taking a break to campaign for Modi. "That image of a guy from 10,000 miles away coming here to pitch for Modi was a great shock to many people. They started trusting me more after they found out about it," says Sharma. He adds that he sometimes got into heated arguments with people over subsidies. "I told them subsidies would keep them poor. Infrastructure and skilling would set them free. I told them, 'If Modi comes, you will get infrastructure and skilling'. Many of them found my arguments convincing though a few of them were very skeptical," he shares.

Sharma's relatives and friends had warned him against areas where regional parties enjoyed massive support, saying it was not safe to canvass for votes for Modi in SP and BSP strongholds. But Sharma had not travelled across the seven seas to play it safe, he decided. "Nothing could stop me from working hard and meeting as many poor people as possible," he says, emphasising that he didn't visit the countryside and small towns in the company of BJP workers because he didn't want to be seen as partisan. "It was my individual effort and the only thing I wanted was to see Modi win," he notes. Sharma went on a whirlwind tour of UP, using locally available forms of transport to get in touch with the people.

The techie created a war room of sorts based out of Noida, UP, by enlisting support from fellow computer specialists who got in touch with people through emails and text messages with appeals to vote for Modi. Many of them would also go door-to-door campaigning to take on the challenge that the Aam Aadmi Party posed in the national capital region. Sharma also approached telecom companies to access phone numbers of people across various "sensitive" states. Sensitive states, to him, were those in which the BJP didn't have much presence. He managed to get volunteers from the US to call these numbers to request a vote for Modi. Many of the recipients of these cold calls slammed the phone, but many others listened patiently. "People were taken aback when someone from the US called and spoke to them in their own language. It left an impression," Sharma claims.

While Sharma decided to hit the campaign trail back home, many others like Narain Kataria, a prominent member of the Indian diaspora in the US and also the director of the pro-Hindu Indian American Intellectuals Forum (IAIF), decided to canvass for votes for Modi while still in the US, by sending across millions of emails and by making thousands of phone calls to Indian voters.

Another Indian-American entrepreneur, Rajiv Malhotra, founder of the pro-Hindu Infinity Foundation who has authored several books including *Breaking India: Western Interventions in Dravidian and Dalit Faultlines,*[1] which he co-authored with Aravindan Neelakandan, says that his contribution to the Modi campaign was through writing blogs online, giving talks, interviewing former AAP volunteers on YouTube, social media, and private canvassing of influential thinkers. "I have also lobbied in the US against the anti-Modi factions for many years," he avers.

Many of these Indian-American Modi admirers also joined hands with eighteen chapters of the Overseas Friends of the BJP (OFBJP) comprising more than 5,000 members across various US cities to organise over 200 tea parties to raise funds for the Modi campaign. Global Indians for Bharat Vikas (GIBV) was also part of the initiative.

Interestingly, there was no noise from pro-Congress overseas bodies such as the Indian National Overseas Congress INOC (I) who seemed inactive ahead of the 2014 elections. The websites of many such organisations showed minimal activity with sporadic updates.

Sensing a victory for Modi, pro-BJP players, on the other hand, also sent many people to work with the BJP in India. What appealed to them, not just in the US, but also in the UK and other countries, besides the Hindutva pull, was Modi's pro-business agenda. Dr Daya Thussu, a professor at the University of Westminster, UK, says, "Pro-market agenda fits very well with the American elite, businesses and corporations. The Indian diaspora is a part of that discourse. In that sense, they are putting Modi forward to the US as someone to do business with." He feels that the diaspora was batting for Modi through media involvement and intellectual discourse. He cites the example of economist Jagdish Bhagwati, who is openly in support of Modi's Gujarat model of development.

At twenty-five million, the India diaspora is not one to be ignored. Except some in the Middle East, most others across the globe were supportive of the Modi campaign through social media and through the use of the Internet and phones.

When quizzed about the role of the Indian diaspora in the elections of 2014, a senior BJP leader told me that raising funds wasn't the primary role of these expats. "Of course, they raised funds, but they are not the golden goose. Golden geese are inside India itself, but overseas Indians help lift the brand of the BJP and Modi. They are sort of opinion leaders (*sic*). If they campaign, people take note. Many of them brought to the table great experience in campaigning through social media and the Internet," he said. "If these NRIs start calling up their relatives and ask them to vote for Modi, it has a greater impact than when relatives back home try to canvass votes. That mode of campaigning was extensively employed this time around."

***

Christophe Jaffrelot has studied the activities of the Rashtra Swayamsevak Sangh abroad. In his book *Religion, Caste and Politics in India*,[2] he tells the interesting story of how two *swayamsevaks* met by chance on a ship and set up a *shakha* abroad. It was in 1946 and the ship was sailing from Bombay to Mombasa in Kenya. They recognised each other as RSS volunteers because both heard each other chanting *Namaste Sada Vatsale Matrubhoome* (Hail Motherland!). The first RSS *shakha* abroad was officially created in 1947 in Kenya by the two ship-bound *swayamsevaks*.

In African countries such as Kenya and Uganda, the RSS named its arms Bharatiya Swayamsevak Sangh, and like the RSS, *shakhas* put a lot of emphasis on physical exercise and cultural activities to foster solidarity among the Hindus. In the US, UK, Canada, the Netherlands, Trinidad and Tobago, RSS operated under the name, Hindu Swayamsevak Sangh. Similarly, Vishwa Hindu Parishad, formed in India in 1964, was set up in the US in 1971 and the UK a year later.

A senior RSS leader concedes that the diaspora was of "extreme help" during the Emergency imposed in India by Indira Gandhi in the June of 1975, which saw civil liberties restricted and elections suspended. The ruling Congress government of the day put pressure on individuals and corporates against funding opposition parties. The "extreme help" he refers to came in the form of an alternative source of funding. With all local sources of financing dried up, opposition leaders either went underground or went abroad – non-resident Indians were benefactors for both.

One of the overseas groups (the Friends of India Society International) even helped publish a magazine, named *Satyavani*, and smuggled it to India. A year or so after the Emergency was lifted in the March of 1977, BJP leader Makarand Desai published a book titled *Smugglers of Truth*,[3] a collection of articles that had appeared in *Satyavani*.

In an interview to Eurotopics.net, great scholar Benedict Anderson talked about a new form of nationalism, which is far more radical than any. "Today we have the long-distance nationalism of those who live in other countries and don't feel they are members of a fully accepted minority in their host nations. They often try to compensate with an exaggerated sense of pride for the country they come from. Mass communication has made this much easier than it once was. People can listen to the radio stations of their home countries, watch DVDs, make telephone calls home, use cheap flights to visit regularly and so on... These people often want to participate in the politics of their countries of origin but don't have to obey the laws or pay the taxes. In a way they're free agents. People who engage in long-distance politics don't have to assume responsibility for its consequences," he said.

The growth of cyber RSS *shakhas* and websites run by overseas Hindu groups that often spew venom on religious minorities and political opponents suggests that Anderson could be right about long-distance nationalism. The websites of these "nationalists" are replete with rabid attacks on the so-called Christian right who they allege lobbied against Modi being given a US visa and silly claims such as that Sonia Gandhi headed a Roman Catholic Church-run government in India. The titles of some workshops held by scholars like Malhotra are also telling. One of them was, *How to be a Hindu Intellectual Kshatriya*.

Oxford University professor Dr Faisal Devji seems to agree with Anderson. Says he: "It is probably true that the diaspora, not having to deal with the messy reality of India, adopts purist and uncompromising positions that can, at times, even include the toleration and incitement to violence. So whereas violence in India itself is still part of a politics of give and take, its diasporic form is much more ideological and pure."

There is a long history of Indians abroad being more "patriotic" than those at home, and even organising militant action against colonial rule – Ghadr being the chief example here, Devji points out. Ghadr was set up in 1913 in the US and Canada to fight for freedom from British rule. "The precedent for more recent funding and support of militancy in India was the Khalistan movement, which was almost entirely driven by the diaspora. The Khalistan movement wanted to create a separate Sikh country within India. The Kashmiris haven't been nearly as successful," adds Devji.

He, however, hastens to add that such violence is not the only contribution by diaspora-nationalism, which also includes genuinely idealistic service for the motherland of the kind celebrated in Bollywood films like *Swades*.

Devji goes on, "Remember, too, that the father of the nation was himself a diasporic Indian, so this history goes back a long way. And yet, unlike Pakistan, whose entire elite and governing class is part of an expatriate population (at least intermittently; the current governor of Punjab in Pakistan, Chaudhry Mohammad Sarwar, for instance, came from Scotland, like one of his colonial predecessors), the Indian diaspora is not (yet) in a position to determine or control the country's future or even present in any serious way."

He adds that if in the colonial period the diaspora represented modernity, wanting to change or revolutionise their motherland in various ways (and this includes Mahatma Gandhi), today it represents, like most diasporas, a conservative force, matching technological progress with traditional family values, as if in an airbrushed form of nostalgia. "Bollywood, which is massively dependent on the diaspora, knows exactly how to represent this world, and it is through Bollywood that the NRI also influences India. In some ways it is only abroad that Hinduism (like Islam) can become a generic and homogeneous phenomenon, since migrants are torn out of their old contexts, and able, in the absence of certain castes, communities, et cetera, to constitute a new kind of Hinduism (and Islam), which then becomes another export back to the motherland," he says, emphasising that it is possibly this sociological condition that also helps the RSS and VHP grow in these places.

***

Prime Minister Modi's ninety-minute address at New York's iconic Madison Square Garden on 28 September 2014 was a stunning hit, with the packed crowd of more than 18,000 people chanting his name and millions of others watching it all over the world. Modi, who was on his regular Navratri fast, was at his oratory best and people didn't seem to bother that he had recycled old jokes (such as how, from being snake charmers, Indians have begun to control the world through the click of a mouse). He received a rock-star welcome nonetheless. In an arena that had previously hosted the likes of Bruce Springsteen, Elvis Presley and Michael Jackson, American senators queued up by Modi's side as he launched into his speech with the slogan, *Bharat Mata ki Jai*. This was a man who until a few months ago was treated like a pariah by the US, which had denied him a visa over the 2002 riots. Twelve years later, however, every utterance Modi made at the venue received loud applause and cheer as he requested Indian-origin entrepreneurs to return to India to help with a showpiece project to bolster local manufacturing, the Make in India programme. He also sought help to clean up the Holy Ganga river. The rapturous welcome he got as he spoke in chaste Hindi only highlighted the unveiling of a rebranding exercise and the support he had among the diaspora ahead of the polls when the members of the community came together to organise tea parties to promote his candidature. The adoring crowds were also enthused by the prospects of Modi steering their home country to the developed-nation status. "Modi's visit to the US was as much about acknowledging and mobilising the diaspora as meeting with American politicians and businessmen, and this is something quite new," opines Devji.

On his return to India, Modi once again stressed the need for tapping foreign talent. He called for keeping a tab on talent pools from each village in the country – the talent pool he was referring

to was about data on each person who has left his or her village
and settled abroad. "We should move ahead keeping this in view.
Every state should set up its own global talent pool. Each state
should set up a global network of its talents wherever in the world
they may be and utilise their experience and talent for the country's
development," Modi said at the Global Investors Summit meet in
Indore on 9 October 2014.

Without doubt, Modi's philosophy in this regard gels well with
the RSS's. In the second week of October, the RSS announced
that it would expand to new countries. For this purpose, RSS
general secretary Dattatreya Hosabale has been visiting European
countries, including Norway, the Netherlands, France, Denmark,
Italy and Finland, among others, to establish branches and
strengthen the Sangh's presence there. In September, Hosabale
had met representatives of different Hindu organisations at the
Swaminarayan temple, Stanmore, London. "Yes, such expansion is
in line with our plans abroad ever since we set up our first branch
in Africa," an RSS leader said. Incidentally, Modi also attracted
immense interest from overseas groups led by industrialists as big
as French-Iranian billionaire Pierre Morad Omidyar, who founded
eBay. He is rumoured to have funded Modi's elections. Jayant Sinha,
a former Omidyar Network partner, is now a junior minister in the
Modi government.

For someone who evokes strong passions as much abroad as at
home, who has had strong links with the diaspora for decades and
has enlisted their support in various campaigns including the 2014
elections, Modi perhaps knows how useful the move could be. Given
the immense success of his branding strategy in just a few months
of coming to power, making him appear one of the most powerful
Asian leaders of this century, the role of the expanding diaspora
base will refine and strengthen his appeal in the international arena.
His thrust on overhauling his image abroad is reminiscent of the
foreign-relations obsessed Pandit Jawaharlal Nehru, the first prime
minister of India who led the country for close to two decades.
The RSS initiative abroad and Modi's 'nationalism' drive is likely
to complement each other. With Modi's constant references to the

2020s at Madison Square Garden and at other forums, he perhaps hopes that he will enjoy Nehru's longevity in power as well. After all, from a polariser to his party's sole proprietor, Modi's survival and growth is undeniably the making of political lore.

The man is firmly in the saddle, but his campaign continues.

Notes

1. Pub. Amaryllis, an imprint of Manjul Publishing House, 2011, Bhopal.
2. Pub. Hurst, 2011, UK.
3. Pub. Friends of India Society International, 1978, India.

EPILOGUE

Candidate Modi was any poll manager's dream. He met all the requirements of a presidential-style candidate in a parliamentary democracy and ploughed his way to victory with seemingly amazing ease. Having ignited the imagination of millions of Indians, many of who became his foot-soldiers in social media during the campaign, he relied on polemic, and his oratorical flourish catapulted him to the extra-large size of a leader-in-waiting. He was stylish, masculine, aggressive and unrelenting. Those qualities, some of which would have looked out of place in normal times, dazzled voters dying for change after a decade-long rule by the Congress-led UPA government in which the prime minister's office, undermined by the ruling party, had long lost its sting and was seen as irresolute. People who had tasted the gains of economic freedom thanks to higher growth in the last decade could not bear the onslaught of the slowdown. The missing leadership of the incumbent gave his rival Modi great advantages as he ripped through traditional strongholds of dynasties and cut through the maze of caste, which often decides victors in Indian politics.

How he overcame caste intricacies and delinked certain castes from their affiliations to certain regional parties, especially in states such as Uttar Pradesh in the general election and in Haryana in the state election held several months later, merits an important mention. As Oxford University professor Dr Faisal Devji suggests, his success could be attributed to "making Hindutva into a public and national phenomenon rather than the product of secret societies, as it had been in the past". By doing so, as he had successfully done in Gujarat earlier, he gave legitimacy to religiosity in a society dominated by secular discourse and, in the process, weakened caste as the single-most important factor that pulled in votes. Perhaps it was a temporary phenomenon, but it helped Modi regardless. As explained earlier, he certainly stood to gain from greater acceptance for the BJP among the backward classes and the Dalits who, over the years, secured greater representation within what was once an upper-class dominated BJP, thanks to a deliberate intra-party strategy of affirmative action.

Maybe author and philosopher Meera Nanda was right about the growing clout of the majority religion in a globalised India. Maybe Modi was a beneficiary of the "intertwining of the Hinduism and neoliberal ideology" that she has explained in detail in her 2010 book, *The God Market*,[1] which argued how, against conventional wisdom, traditional faith had gained greater traction in globalised India and a "state-temple-corporate complex" wielded decisive political and economic power. Hinduism as an economic force with major political and social power is a tempting proposition indeed. Whether or not Modi epitomised that new paradigm, when Modi won, he was seen as the messiah under whose leadership India would forge ahead to glory and super-power status. The hype was in full swing – and it continued at the same pace even months after the 2014 election.

As prime minister, Modi continued to retain the traits of candidate Modi, not letting a single opportunity go waste in campaigning for himself and his party.

He pitched himself as the face of the campaign even after the general election. In a departure from tradition, in the elections to Maharashtra and Haryana state assemblies held in October, he campaigned from the front. Often state elections are fought on local issues where chief ministerial candidates lead the campaigns. Modi was ready to take the risk of being blamed for any reverses that were likely. His gamble paid off. In Haryana, the BJP won a majority and in Maharashtra it became the single-largest party, and he walked away with applause. In both states, the BJP managed to batter dynasties that dominated the political scene to submission. While the Chautalas and the Hoodas were thrashed in Haryana, the Thackerays-led Shiv Sena – a former BJP ally – was humbled in Maharashtra.[2]

The rise of Modi also coincided with what could be a super-cyclical end to fragmentation of Indian polity that started off in the late 1960s when Indira Gandhi installed weak chief ministers to rein in powerful Congress satraps. The long-term outcome of that 'centralisation' effort was the rise of regional parties that cannibalised into the Congress vote base as strong leaders either launched their own parties or weak Congress leadership weakened the party. Pundits aver that Modi, the sole proprietor of his party, could either make the mistakes that Indira Gandhi made or chart out a new course by grooming strong leaders in the states.

Modi's next ambition after bulldozing his way through the Lok Sabha election and state elections is a majority for his party in the Rajya Sabha, the Upper House of Indian Parliament, to push through crucial legislation. He has pinned his hopes on electoral wins in states that would help achieve that goal. The Rajya Sabha will see many members – who are elected by state legislators for a six-year-term – retiring by 2016. The prime minister would be less constrained to push ahead with key bills that may otherwise face roadblocks in the Upper House. Maharashtra and Haryana send twenty-four members to the Rajya Sabha. The party has over the past one year won several state elections, and wrested control of Congress-ruled states like Rajasthan. Which means Modi's efforts to get a majority in the Rajya Sabha is just a matter of time.

Naysayers, meanwhile, say that Modi's hubris following the poll win doesn't bode well for democracy. For instance, some of them highlight important omissions in his exultant speeches celebrating the successful Mars mission, Mangalyaan, the country's first interplanetary mission launched in November 2013, including the fact that he didn't mention the names of the founding fathers of India's space programme. The opposition also alleged that he tried to appropriate credit for the work of the previous government, which launched the Mars mission. But then there are others who believe that as prime minister he is entitled to make such claims in moments of national glory.

Even so, Modi has zealously invoked Congress leaders like Mahatma Gandhi as part of adopting models of leadership from the past. For a celebrated "perpetual slayer of dynasties", Modi has not had qualms in heading the panel that organises the 125th birth anniversary celebrations of Jawaharlal Nehru; he has kept the dynasts away from the committee. Devji offers his reasons about this interesting phenomenon: "He has to adopt his models of leadership from Congress, given the lack of Hindu nationalist leaders in the past who wielded establishment political power. Thus he deploys Indira Gandhi as well as Nehru in his social pronouncements, but never Atal Bihari Vajpayee, interestingly. Patel is invoked a lot but has not yet been 'channelled' by the prime minister in my view, perhaps because he (Patel) had so little time in power."

Such invocations are good enough to lift the mood of the nation. But only briefly. PM Modi's ambitious projects, including the cleanliness drive, his thrust on enhancing indigenous manufacturing and so on, are unlikely to show results unless the government works rigorously towards it. Perfunctory gestures like 'tagging' a handful of political rivals and celebrities on Twitter challenging them to join his Swachh Bharat Mission appear to be simplistic public-relations gimmicks. Such projects require a more comprehensive plan at the grassroots, combining the latest technology with political will. Modi's pronouncement in the run-up to the elections that he plans to build 100 smart cities in India, though lapped up by lakhs of admirers, was seen as a wild exaggeration, if not a joke, by engineers and architects abroad. 'Make in India' is an effort that has been tried out from the time of Prime Minister Nehru, couched in other terms. However noble current Prime Minister Modi's intentions may sound, poor skilling, complex Centre-state relations, low input, waning investor interest, bad quality infrastructure, competition from China, et cetera, are odds that could derail any effort at enhancing India's manufacturing capabilities. Manufacturing contributed only 13 percent to India's GDP in 2013, according to World Bank data – lower than corresponding figures in Pakistan and Bangladesh, not to mention BRIC countries. India is not yet hot for global manufacturing giants, which have other easier options to make products – for many of them India now figures only as an export market. The closure of the Nokia mobile-phone making unit near Chennai is a wake-up call. Poor strategy by the Finnish company was one major reason for the shutdown. There are others though, including confrontation with tax men and Indian bureaucracy, and militant trade unionism.

Certainly, a lot more needs to be done to hard-sell 'Make in India' than mere PowerPoint presentations by smart, well-dressed bureaucrats and an attractive website created by some of the best graphic artists in town.

Besides, any politics that plays on creating insecurity among the minorities and smacks of polarising tactics – something that was observed in poll-bound states before and after the general election – bodes ill for a democracy.

The people have given Narendra Modi the mandate, more than anything else, to be a true democrat and a doer. As the consummate politician and survivor, Modi knows that hoopla and hype can only take him so far. The opportunity is ripe for him to use his prowess as a game-changer and campaigner in the governance of a nation of 1.2 billion people. If he can pull this off, he would go down in history as one of the strongest reformers the country has seen.

Notes

1. Pub. Monthly Review Press, 2012.
2. The Chautala family heads the Indian National Lok Dal (INLD), comprising scions of the late farmer leader and former Deputy Prime Minister Devi Lal. His son and former Haryana Chief Minister Om Prakash Chautala, grandsons and great grandsons are active in politics. Bhupinder Hooda, son of the late freedom fighter Ranbir Hooda, is a former chief minister of Haryana. His son and daughter are active in state politics. Shiv Sena was founded by the late Balasaheb Thackeray and his family wields enormous clout in Maharashtra state politics.

ACKNOWLEDGEMENTS

I would like to thank Roli Books for giving me the opportunity to write this book. I am also grateful to PR Ramesh, managing editor of OPEN magazine, for his unstinting support and generous inputs, and to S Prasannarajan, editor of OPEN magazine, for his faith and patience.

This book would also not have been possible without the help and cooperation of the numerous interviewees who gave me hours of their time, from politicians and party workers to social-media wizards, poll managers and grassroots volunteers.

Most notably, I would like to thank Dharmendra Pradhan, Minister of State for Petroleum and Natural Gas, for his extensive guidance that was critical to my research, and Piyush Goyal, Minister of State with Independent Charge for Power, Coal and New & Renewable Energy, who gave me invaluable minutes of his time in the height of the election campaign. I am also grateful to Dr Vijay Chauthaiwale for sharing a war-room insider's perspective, and top-notch adman Piyush Pandey for a long evening and hospitality at his home.

Thanks are also due to my editor Renuka Chatterjee for her keen eye and insightful questions, and to my friends Anil Kumar of the *Economic Times*, Siddharth Singh at MINT newspaper, and CP Surendran, editor-in-chief of DNA newspaper, for their tips and encouragement. Cheers also to John Brittas, Praveen Thampi, Dinesh Narayanan and Sumedh Rajendran for keeping me in good spirits!

And, of course, at the end and always is my wife Aekta Kapoor, my partner in time.

BIBLIOGRAPHY

How Modi's name was cleared for campaign chief and PM (story by PR Ramesh). http://www.openthemagazine.com/article/nation/it-was-a-faith-accompli Details of the BJP-RSS organisational apparatus in Varanasi for the poll. http:// timesofindia.indiatimes.com/city/lucknow/Two-Sangh-leaders-to-oversee-BJP-functioning-in-the-state/articleshow/28694388.cms

2004 poll defeat. http://www.theguardian.com/world/2004/may/14/india. randeepramesh

Six-year banishment as opportunity. http://timesofindia.indiatimes.com/ news/Six-year-banishment-led-to-Narendra-Modis-metamorphosis/ articleshow/33040649.cms?

Vajpayee's Rajdharma speech; Modi interrupts. https://www.youtube.com/ watch?v=x5W3RCpOGbQ

Scams under UPA. http://indiatoday.intoday.in/gallery/upa-govt-9-years-9-scams-sonia-manmohan/4/9401.html

AAP: High on Hype? http://www.openthemagazine.com/article/nation/aap-high-on-hype

Diaspora and Modi in 2014 polls. http://www.aljazeera.com/indepth/ features/2014/04/us-groups-overseas-funds-modi-2014417102320868846. html

RSS to open more shakhas overseas. http://www.sunday-guardian.com/news/rss-will-open-shakhas-abroad

Vibhuti Agarwal's piece on the Ishrat Jahan case. http://blogs.wsj.com/ indiarealtime/2013/07/05/the-ishrat-jahan-case-an-explainer/

Modi's political Run for Unity. http://www.ndtv.com/article/india/narendra-modi-s-political-run-for-unity-ahead-of-2014-elections-458939

Gujarat promises all-round progress: Bhagwati & Panagariya. http://articles. economictimes.indiatimes.com/2013-01-02/news/36111596_1_kerala-model-gujarat-model-social-indicators

Delhi gang-rape case. http://zeenews.india.com/news/nation/delhi-gang-rape-case-sc-stays-execution-of-vinay-sharma-akshay-thakur_947295.html

INDEX

2G scam, 111-112
3D hologram campaign/rallies, 4, 47, 68-71, 73, 76
  managing of, 71
  success of, 70-71

Aam Aadmi Party (AAP), 16, 17, 66, 109, 110, 112, 122-125, 129
  win in Delhi polls, 123-124
Abki baar Modi sarkar campaign, 41, 42, 44-46
  popularity of, 45
Achche din aanewale hain line, 46
Adani, Gautam, 101
Adarsh Housing Society scam, 110, 111
Adi Shankara, 7, 87
Advani, LK, 13-15, 33, 59, 91, 92, 95, 97, 102, 103
Aga, Anu, 101
Agarwal, Naresh, 60
Aiyar, Mani Shankar, 1, 60
  comment on Modi, 60
Akhil Bharatiya Vidhyarti Parishad (ABVP), 25, 27
Ambani, Anil, 101, 103
Ambani, Dhirubhai, 102
Ambani, Mukesh, 101
Amin, Hasiba B, 67
Anderson, Benedict, 131
Ansari, Mukhtar, 16
Anti-Sikh riots (of 1984), 95-96
APCO Worldwide, 56-58, 101
Apna Dal, 21, 23, 33
Arab Spring, 53, 108, 110
Asom Gana Parishad, 124
Assembly elections of November 2013, 120
Asterix Solutions, 127
Avaaz.org, 108-109
  criticism of, 108

Babri Mosque, 9, 31, 83

  demolition of, 31, 83
Babu Bajrangi, 98
Bachchan, Amitabh, 38
Bajpai, Laxmikant, 69, 70, 73
Bansal, Sunil, 25, 26,73
Bhagalpur riots in 1989, 96
Bhagwat, Madhukar Rao, 94
Bhagwat, Mohan, 11-13, 94,
Bhagwati, Jagdish, 57, 58, 115, 116, 129
  supporting Modi's Gujarat model, 57, 129
Bharat Vijay rallies, 78-80
  preparations of, 79-80
Bhartiya Janta Party (BJP),
  advertising blitzkrieg of, 37
  election committees of, 49
  in Maharashtra, 35
  and Shiv Sena ties, 34
Bharatiya Swayamsevak Sangh, 130
Bharti, Uma, 22, 23
Bhatele, Gaurav, 52, 53, 55
Bhuj earthquake of 2001, 94
Birla, Kumar Mangalam, 101
Bofors arms deal, 11
Bombay riots in 1992, 96
Bose, Sumantra, 122, 123

Captain Abhimanyu, 25
Cash-for-vote scam, 110
Centre Right India (CRI), 67
Chai pe Charcha campaign, 60-61, 63-65, 68, 71, 73, 76
  at Assi Ghat, 62-65
  impact of, 65
Chaudhary, Shankarbhai, 22
Chauhan, Shankarbhai, 109
Chauhan, Shivendra Singh, 109
Chauhan, Shivraj, 14
Chaurasia, Rameshwar, 25
Chauthaiwale, Dr. Vijay, 20, 21, 23, 25, 44, 60, 75, 76, 79, 141
Chavan, Ashok, 111

Chhibber, Pradeep, 124
Chidambaram, P, 107
Citizens for Accountable Governance
    (CAG), 53-56, 58-64, 70-73, 76-81
    data-analytics' strategy of, 77-78
    the first major event of, 54
    pre-poll interviews of, 80
    social listening concept of, 80-81
    support Modi campaign, 58-60
Coal corruption, 111-112
Cobrapost.com, 27
Commonwealth Games (CWG) scandal,
    110, 111
Congress,
    campaign machinery, 65-68
    and Mein Nahin Hum slogan, 66

Daisy Girl ad, 42
Dasgupta, Swapan, 69
Delhi gangrape case, 111-114
    and public outrage, 112-114
Delhi the 'rape capital', 113
Delhi war room, 20-21, 79
Dentsu ad agency, 66
Deoras, Balasaheb, 20
Desai, Makarand, 131
    Smugglers of Truth, 131
Deshpande, Haima, 89
Devi, Rabri, 81
Devji, Faisal, 131-133, 137, 139
Dikshit, Sheila, 16, 113, 123
Dixit, Neha, 29
Dreze, Jean, 119
Dutt, Priya, 80

Election Commission, 29, 32, 36, 50, 69
Eligible voters, 3
    in Uttar Pradesh, 3
Eurotopics.net, 131

Ficha Limpa protests, 108, 122

Gadkari, Nitin, 13, 49, 94
Gandhi, Indira, 11, 90, 95, 103, 105, 130,
    138, 139
Gandhi, Mahatma, 55, 59, 81, 108, 132, 139
    assassination of, 31, 59
Gandhi, Rahul, 5, 36, 66-68, 70, 71, 79, 82,
    113, 120-122, 124, 125
    amateur politics of, 121
    interview on Times Now, 66
    as shehzaada, 67, 121

tagged as Pappu, 122
Gandhi, Rajiv, 11, 95, 99
    assassination of, 99
Gehlot, Thawarchand, 13
General election in 2014, 3, 4, 8, 21, 51, 90,
    119, 121, 129, 134
    electronic gloss and glamour in, 4
    presidential by nature, 4, 40, 50, 55, 56,
    66, 75
Genesis Burson-Marsteller, 66
Ghadr, 132
Gill, SS, 31
Global Indians for Bharat Vikas (GIBV), 129
Global Investors Summit, 134
Global slowdown, 114
Godhra train carnage, 56-57, 83-85, 96, 98
Godse, Nathuram, 31
Golden Dawn, 54
Goldwater, Barry, 42
Golwalkar, Madhav Sadashiv, 10
Google Hangout, 4, 60, 61
Gopal, Dr Krishna, 15
Gopinath, Gita, 114
Goyal, Piyush, 39, 40, 43, 49, 51, 67, 141
    poll campaigner for Modi, 43-46
    people working with, 46
Greynisum Information Technologies, 75
Gujarat model, 57, 127, 129
Gujarat riots in 2002, 13, 16, 17, 32, 41, 57,
    58, 69, 84-86, 95-102, 133
    Caravan report on, 100
Gujarat Tourism commercials, 38-39, 48
Gulail.com, 27
Gulbarg Society, 85
Gupta, Arvind, 50, 76
Gupta, Dipankar, 31
Gupta, Shyama Charan, 23

Har Har Modi campaign, 8
Hashimpura riots in 1987, 96
Hazare, Kisan Baburao "Anna", 74, 106, 122
    agitation in 2011, 107-110, 122-123
    hunger strike by, 106
    in jail, 107
    most influential persons of 2011, 107
Hedgewar, Dr Keshav Baliram, 10
Heeraben (Modi's mother), 86, 89
Hooda, Bhupinder, 66, 138, 140
Hosabale, Dattatreya, 134

Inamdar, Lakshmanrao, 92

India Against Corruption (IAC), 74, 106-110, 122
    missed call campaign of, 74
    success of, 106
India Behind The Lens (IBTL), 67
India272.com, 76
Indian American Intellectuals Forum (IAIF), 128
Indian diaspora, 128-130, 132
    patriotism of, 132
    role in 2014 elections, 129
India-US civil nuclear deal, 119
IndiaWorld, 74
Indo-Pakistan War of 1971, 90
Institute of Applied Manpower Research (IAMR), 118
Iris Business Services report 2013, 60
Ishrat Jahan encounter case, 27, 35

Jabalpur riots in 1961, 31
Jadvekar, Prakash, 40
Jaffrelot, Christophe, 85, 130
    Religion, Caste and Politics in India, 130
Jafri, Ehsan, 85
Jain, Nilesh, 46
Jain, Rajesh, 74, 76
    criticism of, 76
    role in Modi's digital media team, 75
Jaitley, Arun, 11, 13, 33, 40, 43, 46, 49
Jalan, Piyush, 53
Janta maaf nahin karegi campaign, 41
Jha, Nandan, 53
Jha, Rajkumar, 46
Jinping, Xi, 87
Johnson, Lyndon, 42
Joshi, Bhaiyyaji, 13
Joshi, Murli Manohar, 14-15, 26, 49, 91, 104
    and his Ekta Yatra, 91
Joshi, Prasoon, 45
Joshi, Sanjay, 92-94
    Modi's hostilities with, 93-94
Kalam, Abdul, 54
Kaplan, Robert D., 58
Kataria, Narain, 128
Kauser Bi, 27
Kejriwal, Arvind, 16-18, 66, 67, 106, 109, 110, 122, 123, 125
    as Delhi chief minister, 125
    launched AAP, 109, 110
Khalistan movement, 132
Khandelwal, Anuraag, 46

Khurshid, Salman, 107, 120
Kishor, Prashant, 53, 55, 56, 58, 61, 76, 81
    meeting with Modi, 55
    Modi's Man Friday, 53
    youth force of, 55-56
Kodnani, Maya, 98
Kumar, Devendra, 12
Kumar, UK Senthil, 68
Kushwaha, Satyendra, 25

Ladwa, Manoj, 25, 43, 44, 79
Le Pen, Marine, 54
Lenin, 123

Madison Square Garden, New York, 7, 126, 133, 135
    PM Modi's address at, 133
Mahajan, Poonam, 49, 80
Mahajan, Pramod, 34, 35, 40
Mahatma Gandhi National Rural Employment Generation Act (MGNREGA), 119
Mahesh, BG, 75
Make in India programme, 133, 139, 140
Malhotra, Rajiv, 129
Malini, Hema, 24
Mangalyaan Mars mission, 138
Manthan campaign, 54-56, 58
Marino, Andy, 89, 92, 94, 96, 97
    Narendra Modi: A Political Biography, 89
Marx, Karl, 123
Modi Aane Wala Hain (MAWH) campaign, 71-73
    key priorities of, 72-73
Mayawati, 10, 30, 127
Miliband, Ed, 51
Mishra, Kalraj, 23
Mitta, Manoj, 95, 99
    When a Tree Shook Delhi: The 1984 Carnage and its Aftermath, 95
Mittal, Sunil, 101, 102
Modi , Damodardas Mulchand (Modi's father), 86
Modi team, poll commercials of, 36-37
Modi wave, 18, 52, 53
Modi, Narendra,
    accusations after 2002 riots on, 56-57, 85-86, 98-101
    active member of RSS, 89-90
    ad man's delight, 46
    as BJP's prime ministerial candidate, 8, 13

as chief campaigner of the BJP, 13-14
chief minister of Gujarat, 12, 95,101
childhood of, 86-87
as general secretary of BJP, 93, 95
image overhauling of, 57-60
married, 88
Muslim fear for, 17-18
plaudits to, 102
presidential-style candidate, 136
prime ministerial nominee, 14, 15
Public Enemy Number One, 56
reelected CM in 2012, 101
riots-tainted image of, 56-60
visit to the US, 133
Modi, Jashoda Chimanlal (Jashoda), 88-90
Moveon.org, 108
Mukherjee, Abhijit, 113
Munde, Gopinath, 34, 35, 49
Murti, NR Narayana, 101
Muzaffarnagar riots, 29-32

Nadda, JP, 44
Naidu, N Venkaiah, 13, 61
NaMo number campaign, 75
NaMo versus RaGa fight, 67
Nanda, Meera, 137
    The God Market, 137
Naqvi, Mukhtar Abbas, 50
Narayan, Badri, 23
Narayan, Jayaprakash, 53, 91, 103, 105
Naroda Patiya massacre, 85, 98
Nussbaum, Martha C., 57, 86
Natarajan, Jayanthi, 117
National Advisory Council (NAC), 116
National Democratic Alliance (NDA), 10,
    13, 40, 41, 79, 101
Nationalist Congress Party (NCP), 35
Naxalbari movement, 53
Neelakandan, Aravindan, 129
Nehru, Pandit Jawaharlal, 36, 82, 88, 105,
    120, 134, 135, 139
Netcore Solutions, 74, 76
Nussbaum, Martha C, 57, 86

Obama, Barack, 51
October Revolution of Russia, 123
Ogilvy and Mather (O&M), 38
Ogilvy, David, 38, 43, 48
Omidyar, Pierre Morad, 134
Overseas Friends of the BJP (OFBJP), 129
Pal, Jagadambika, 23

Panagariya, Arvind, 57, 58, 115, 117
Pandey, Piyush, 36-48, 141
    first political campaign of, 37-38
    working for Maharashtra polls, 48
Parekh, Deepak, 101
Paris Commune, 123
Patel, Anandiben, 26
Patel, Anupriya, 21
Patel, Keshubhai, 92-94
Patel, Sardar Vallabhbhai, 59, 105
Patel, Dr Sone Lal, 21
Pawar, Sharad, 35
Phoolka, HS, 95
Poorna Swaraj movement, 53
Pradhan, Dharmendra, 15,73, 81, 141
Prajapati, Tulsiram, 27
Prakash, Om, 79
Prasad, Lalu, 81
Prasad, Ravi Shankar, 49

Radia, Niira, 102
Raghavan, RK, 99
    Gujarat investigations by, 99
Rai, Ajay, 8, 16, 18
Raja, Andimuthu, 111
Rajosana Primary School, 89
Ram Janmabhoomi agitation, 9, 31, 53
Ram, Kanshi, 21
Ramakrishna, R, 36, 50
Ramesh, Jairam, 117
Ramesh, PR, 14
Rana, Suresh, 29
Rao, NT Rama, 124
Rao, PV Narasimha, 12, 91, 116
Rashtriya Swayam Sevak Sangh (RSS), 10-
    18, 20, 27, 33, 47, 50, 58, 59, 74, 77, 78,
    86-88, 90-92, 94, 109, 130, 131, 133, 134
    cyber shakhas of, 131
    founding of, 10
    initiative abroad, 130, 134
    shakhas of, 10
Rawat, Trivendra, 25
Res Publica, 108
Right to Information Act (RTI), 90, 120
Rudy, Rajiv Pratap, 49, 81
Run for Unity project, 59

Sabarmati Express, 83, 96
    burning of, 83, 96
Satyavani, 131
Scroll.in, 29, 74

Shah, Amit, 14, 15, 19-35, 40, 43, 49, 73, 92
  a constant troubleshooter, 24-25
  life of, 19-20
  as president of the BJP, 29,
  plannings in UP, 19-35
  political career of, 28-29
  a tainted politician, 27-29
Shah, Anilchandra, 19
Shahi, Surya Pratap, 23
Shakur, Tupac, 69
Sharma, Amitabh, 127-128
  work among Dalits in UP, 127
  campaigning for Modi, 127
Sharma, Shrikant, 24
Sharma, Supriya, 74
Sheikh, Sohrabuddin, 27
Sherawat, Manish, 46
Shinde, Sushil, 113
Shining India campaign, 40, 41
Shiv Sena, 34-35, 138, 140
Sibal, Kapil, 107
Sidhu, Navjot Singh, 49
Singh, Ajit, 30, 31
Singh, Charan, 31
Singh, Digvijaya, 97
Singh, Hridyanath, 25
Singh, Kalyan, 24
Singh, Kirti Vardhan, 23
Singh, Manmohan, 66, 106, 110-112, 115-117
  crisis in the government of, 111
Singh, Rajnath, 11, 14, 29, 40, 59
Singh, Raman, 14, 15, 19, 27, 40, 43, 49,
  73, 92
Singh, Ranveer, 24
Singh, Rishi Raj, 25, 52
Singhal, GL, 27
Sinha, Jayant, 134
Sinha, Mukesh, 76
Sinha, Pratik, 76
Sircar, Shoojit, 46
Sitharaman, Nirmala, 40, 41, 43
Soho Square, 38, 41, 42, 46
  first campaign of, 41
Soni, Pranlal, 28
Soni, Suresh, 13
State of Emergency in India, 11, 90-92, 103-
  105, 130, 131
Statue of Unity Movement (SOUM), 58-59
  social mobilization mandate of, 59
Subramaniam, Chitra, 11
Surat riots in 1993, 96

Swachh Bharat Mission, 139
Swami Atmasthananda, 89
Swaraj, Sushma, 13, 40, 49, 103

Tata, Ratan, 57, 101, 102
Team Modi, 5, 22, 45, 78
  volunteers enlisted by, 5
Telegu Desam Party (TDP), 124
Thackeray, Balasaheb, 34
Thackery, Uddhav, 34, 35
Thakre, Kushabhau, 91
The Economic Times, 14, 101, 109, 124
Thussu, Dr Daya, 129
Tikait, Mahendra Singh, 30
Tripathi, Kamalapati, 9, 23
Tripathi, Kesri Nath, 23
TruthOfGujarat.com, 76
Tsang, Hiuen, 86, 87
Tyagi, KC, 59

Udayabhanu, Prem, 85
United Progressive Alliance (UPA), 11, 12,
  41, 42, 49, 79, 106, 107, 110, 111, 114-
  117, 119, 120, 136
  corruption charges on, 111-112, 115-119
  decline of, 115-117
  during first and second terms, 114-118
  jobless growth during, 118

Vadnagar, 60, 86-88, 90
Vaghela, Shankersinh, 91-94
  exit from BJP, 92-93
Vajpayee, AB, 13, 40, 42, 93, 94, 97, 99,
  116, 139
Vajpayee, Abeer, 48
Varanasi, 7-9, 11, 13-18, 26, 53, 58, 62, 77,
  87, 125
  holi festival at, 7-8
  as Modi's constituency, 14-15
  upper-caste politics at, 9
Verma Commission, 99
Vibrant Gujarat summit, 56, 57, 101, 102
Vishwa Hindu Parishad, 130
Vodafone case, 116

World Hindu Organisation, 127

Yadav, Chandrapal, 22
Yadav, Mulayam Singh, 9, 32, 70, 132
Yadav, Ramkripal, 81
Young India conference, 54